KT-118-656

THE ART OF
MARBLING

THE ART OF
MARBLING

Stuart Spencer

Macdonald Orbis

A **Macdonald Illustrated** BOOK

© Macdonald & Co Ltd 1988

First published in Great Britain in 1988
by Macdonald & Co (Publishers) Ltd
London & Sydney

A member of Maxwell Macmillan Pergamon Publishing Corporation

1st Reprint 1990
2nd Reprint 1990
Text copyright © Stuart Spencer
Illustrations copyright © Macdonald & Co

All rights reserved
No part of this publication may be reproduced, stored in a retrieval
system, or transmitted, in any form or by any means without the
prior permission in writing of the publisher, nor be otherwise
circulated in any form of binding or cover other than that in which it
is published and without a similar condition including this condition
being imposed on the subsequent purchaser.

British Library Cataloguing in Publication Data
Spencer, Stuart
Marbling.
1. Marbling
I. Title
745.7'2   TT323

ISBN 0-356-15328-2

Filmset by SX Composing Ltd
Colour Separation by Kwong Ming Graphicprint, Hong Kong
Printed and bound in Great Britain
by BPCC Paulton Books Limited

Senior Editor: Judith More
Editor: John Wainwright
Art Editor: Simon Webb
Designer: Annie Tomlin
Photographer: Jon Bouchier
Indexer: Margaret Cooter

Macdonald & Co (Publishers) Ltd
Orbit House
1 New Fetter Lane
London EC4A 1 AR

CONTENTS

INTRODUCTION

When we decorate our homes we continue a tradition the origins of which may be traced back some thirty thousand years, to the cave paintings of our earliest ancestors. Their achievements reflect not only the dawning of man's creative spirit, but also his desire to capture the colours and forms of the natural world, and to create them in the comparative safety of what must have been his first permanent home. While modern decoration may have little to do with warding off evil spirits or placating ancient Gods, the home, like the cave, remains a sanctuary; not against wild animals or fierce adversaries, but against the anonymity of an ever more impersonal world. By surrounding ourselves with familiar objects and reassuring colours we construct environments that not only reflect our characters and personalities, but also demonstrate our practical skills and artistic abilities.

The Pantheon, a circular temple dedicated to all gods, was built in Rome by Agrippa in 25 BC. It was restored by Hadrian in AD 120, and has been in use as a Christian church since 609. Marble was used extensively as a building stone and decorative material in its construction. The scale and grandeur of such monuments and the quality of design, craftsmanship and skill that went into erecting them have done much to forge our traditional response to marble, popularly acknowledged as the most prestigious of all building materials.

In order to understand something of the revival of interest in decorative painting, and indeed the whole crafts movement, we must look to the disenchantment felt by many people with the realities of the materialistic world in which they live.

While advertising and the media generate a buoyant market place, our tastes are manipulated and our appetites cloned with a cynicism that stifles individual choice and produces a treadmill of endless fashion up-dates and trivial styles.

Equally, whilst modern methods of production provide us with a vast range of competitively priced goods and services, their quality and standard often leave much to be desired. The hand of the craftsman has been priced out of the design equation, and in consequence we must look back to a more sympathetic past for his presence and our inspiration.

For instance, a typical Egyptian town, Kahin, dating back to 1900 BC, showed the homes of workers to be decorated with brown skirtings and blue, red and white striped walls, topped with buff areas containing brightly coloured panels. Similarly the ruins of Pompeii and Herculaneum, perfectly preserved by volcanic ash, reveal brightly coloured domestic interiors, often depicting detailed murals of plays or rural scenes, usually finished with a lustrous wax to simulate the decorative stone, marble. During the era of Louis XIV and the Rococo style, interiors were vibrant with greens and lilacs, pinks and whites, and yellows and silvers, adorning the walls in a style that echoed the widespread use of marble in fixtures and fittings. This approach found expression in England in the more formal, yet equally elegant, Palladian style. Just these few examples from a rich heritage of decorative embellishment and ornamentation, present us with an alternative to the current preoccupation with essentially impersonal, unbroken expanses of pale pastels and off-whites.

Traditionally, it has been paint that has provided us with the most practical method of decorating our homes. While technology continually improves the quality and variety of paint, its versatility as a decorative tool is exploited through the vision and talent of artists, painters and craftsmen. With the current popular demand for information, that versatility, and the secrets of the professional decorative painter, have been revealed. Not only are the materials they use readily available in retail stores, but the techniques themselves are easily mastered by anyone who can follow simple instructions and wield a paint brush.

These techniques and materials, initially borrowed from the fine artist, have been formalised and refined over the centuries into various disciplines known as 'broken colour techniques'. Fundamental to each of them is the use

The ancient Italian city of Pompeii, situated south-east of Naples, was buried when the volcano Vesuvius erupted in AD 79. Volcanic ash preserved much of the city intact, and thanks to painstaking archaeological excavation we are permitted a glimpse into the cultural and artistic achievements of a refined society. While exotic murals such as the one illustrated below demonstrate the skills of the artisans, it is perhaps more revealing to note that the homes of common citizens were often decorated in a most colourful and unreserved fashion.

This vast perspective mural of Rome, painted by Peruzzi, occupies a wall in the Villa Farnesina. The artists and craftsmen of the Renaissance often sought inspiration in the classical disciplines of antiquity. The skill with which the artist draws us into the spacial illusion can, for our purposes, be surpassed only by his ability to simulate the beautiful breche marble colonnade.

of paint, in the form of a glaze. This thin coat of transparent colour lies at the very heart of decorative painting, and the manner in which it is applied to the surface gives rise to the names of the various techniques. Hence 'sponging', for example, describes the pattern produced when a glaze is dabbed on to a surface, and 'dragging' involves pulling a fine brush through the wet glaze. Although these techniques produce recognised finishes in their own right, it is only when we combine them that we are able to enter the fascinating world of 'marbling'.

As interest has once more focused on the painted illusion, marbling, above all others, seems to have seized the

prestigious of all building materials. So powerful is this association that the merest hint of a blurred, diagonal vein is sufficient to evoke an immediate impression of solidity, formality, integrity and opulence. Consequently, given that the logistics of handling the stone have always proved financially restricting, the handiwork of the decorative painter, and his attempts to simulate the extraordinary qualities of the polished stone, are to be found throughout history.

This book will concentrate on the simulation of various types of marble in paint. However, it must be remembered that as an illusory technique marbling is essentially a decorative tool; a means to an end, rather than an end in itself. Consequently, in order to help you to develop and exploit the full potential of marbling in your home, part of the text will be devoted to the discussion of such topics as colour, scale, proportion and even 'good taste'. You should always consider these points carefully before you embark on your marbling scheme.

Finally, whilst recognising that there can be no substitute for experience, the most important requirements for any newcomer to the world of marbling are enthusiasm, imagination and, above all, a sense of humour. Whilst you should not expect to meet with *instant* success, if you adopt a patient methodical approach, and you follow carefully the simple step-by-step marbling techniques we have laid down, you will be pleasantly surprised at how quickly and easily a marble will appear before your eyes.

But do remember, a light-hearted approach is essential too, if you are to produce marbling that is not merely a dull copy, but rather, a lively, spirited and unique effect.

attention of the general public. Its impact is founded on the powerful psychological link that exists between the instantly recognisable visual signature of marble, and our own experience of the traditional manner and situations in which it is used; namely, that over the centuries marble has established itself as the most decorative and

MARBLE AND MARBLING

Within the field of marbling there is a statement often bandied about: 'If in need of guidance or inspiration, always consult the natural stone'. This is sound advice, as it will be seen that the strength of any painted illusion relies heavily on a familiarity with the stone and its traditional areas of use.

Rhodochrosite is a highly prized, manganese-bearing mineral that reveals beautiful colours when cut and polished. This crystallized example can give little indication of the beautiful banded strata that emerge when the stone is processed.

MARBLE – THE SHINING STONE

The term 'Marble' derives from the Greek word for 'shining stone'. Embodied within this charming understatement lies not only the most revered of all building materials, but also one of the most stunning visual displays to be found in our world. Locked within the very rocks beneath our feet are, literally, the patterns and colours of creation itself.

While the use of marble predates recorded history, it was during the classical periods of the Greek and Roman civilisations that its potential was fully

On the polished stone the banded strata of processed Rhodochrosite are fully in evidence. The original rough crystal, when cut and polished, refines into a spectacular amalgam of jagged yellow, crimson and white veins.

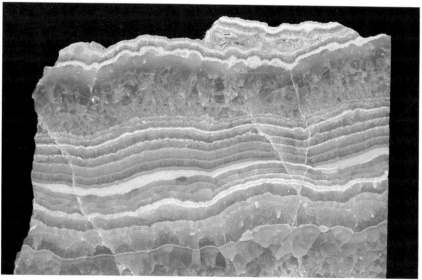

exploited. The popular vision of classicism is one of large expanses of masonry, with clean, unadorned surfaces. However, this is something of a myth. In order to counteract the bleaching effect of the brilliant Mediterranean sun, the Greeks reinforced the elegant proportions of their ceremonial buildings and magnificent statues with flamboyant painted decoration, and inlay work executed in all manner of polished stone, carved ivory and gold leaf.

Subsequently, the Romans embraced Greek architecture, interpreting it on a massive scale. However, Greek embellishment was considered trivial, and it was replaced with the more formal and, for them, aesthetically pleasing material, marble; a stone found in great variety and abundance, literally in their own back yard. Augustus Caesar was said to have 'found Rome brick and left it marble'.

The essential character of marble had been established, so that nowadays whether it be found in the cathedrals of Northern Europe, the facades of modern banks or the foyers of prestigious hotels, its presence is always synonymous with formality and opulence.

The geology of marble

Marble is the collective, commercial name given to 'any rock whose surface is capable of taking a decorative polish'. Whilst this definition will suffice for our purposes, in order for us to adopt a systematic approach to examining the decorative stones that we may wish to simulate, it is advisable to have a grasp of the way in which rocks are formed, identified and named.

can produce stress fractures in the structure of the rock, allowing acidic fluids to percolate through them, taking the path of least resistance, to produce new minerals, each with its own distinctive colour and crystalline structure. It is these veins, which stand out in sharp contrast to their background, which are the most dramatic, expressive and immediately recognisable signature of marble.

Rocks are divided into three separate geological categories: Igneous, Metamorphic and Sedimentary. Each of these groups contains a number of decorative stones.

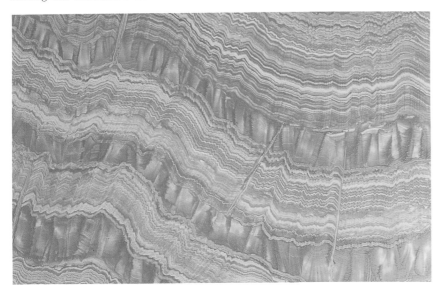

The parallel banding in Rhodochrosite can be easily simulated (see page 122), and this makes it a favourite for fantasy techniques. It is also very effective for wall panelling systems, but care must be taken to see that it does not dominate the surrounding decor.

Petrology

This is the study of the forces responsible for the creation of the various rocks that evolve, over millions of years, within the earth's crust. These forces, vast pressures and high temperatures are reflected in the visual appearance of rock. For example, the forces

Igneous rocks

These are formed when molten magma, a viscous soup of melted rock, cools and solidifies. Typical of this group are the granites and porphyries that are seen as facing stones on many banks and public buildings. As a rule they are displayed as a uniformly patterned material, with few structural imperfections.

Sedimentary rocks

These cover about two-thirds of the earth's surface and are formed when

The inlaid marble table shown left has a lapis lazuli centre and an outermost circle of verde antico. The other marbles on its surface are listed in the chart opposite, starting clockwise from the top of each ring (for ring order see the key above).

This table top is decorated with fragments of polished marble that were discovered during excavation work carried out around the Appian Way immediately outside Rome. The simple mosaic pattern indicates how easily and effectively marbles may be combined to create a decorative theme.

sediment, composed of old, weathered rocks and the skeletons of small animals, is welded together under pressure. During this process, new minerals are often formed to produce all manner of decorative stones, such as breccias, fossiliverous and variegated limestones, travertines, gypsums, and alabasters. Their patterning and colour reveal tremendous variations, and they are used extensively within the home for surfaces, furniture and artefacts.

Metamorphic rocks

These are produced when heat and pressure combine to recrystalise existing rocks, without actually causing them to melt. This category contains the classification 'marble', the purest varieties of which are composed almost entirely of recrystalised limestone. The most famous marbles are the white statuary varieties, found in the Carrara Mountains of Italy. No other sculpting material so accurately captures the

CIRCLE A	Giallo antico • Cipollino • Onyx marble • Serpentine • Cottanello • Onyx marble • Bardiglio • Onyx marble • African • Breccia dorata • Onyx marble • African • Breccia dorata • Porta Santa • Lumachella • Stellania • Pavonazzetto • Lumachella (*Fine marble*) • Onyx marble • Onyx marble • Onyx marble • Breccia traccagnia • Breccia • Porfido serpentino • Onyx marble • Breccia corallina • Onyx marble • Onyx marble • Onyx marble • Broccatello de Tortosa • Pietra nefritica • Amethyst • Broccatello de Tortosa • Onyx marble • Lumachella
CIRCLE B	Grannito rosso • Breccia di Susa • Africano rosso • Onyx marble (*Alabastro di Palombara*) • Broccatello de Tortosa • Onyx marble (*Alabastro di Orta*) • Breccia di Serravezza persichina • Onyx marble (*Alabastro fiorito*) • Pietra nefritica • Breccia di Tivoli • Calcite • Africano chiaro • Sette Basi • Onyx marble • Lumachella pavonazza • Onyx marble (*Alabastro a nuvole*) • Malachite • Breccia di Cori • Semesanto • Broccatello de Tortosa • Calcite • Onyx marble (*Alabastro a occhi*) • Onyx marble (*Alabastro a rosa*) • Rosso brecciato • Leocite tephrite • Onyx marble • Semesanto • Onyx marble • Breccia ombrata • Onyx marble (*Alabastro ragato*) • Pavesina (*Ruin marble*) • Sette Basi
CIRCLE C	Onyx marble • Africano minuto • Onyx marble (*Alabastro rigato*) • Onyx marble (*Alabastro rosso*) • Agrignana • Giallo antico • Granito del Foro Trajano • Calcite • Onyx marble • Fior di persico • Cipollino verde • Cipollino pavonazzo • Onyx marble • Breccia corallina • Breccia di Cori • Breccia • Onyx marble (*Alabastro rigato*) • Onyx marble • Onyx marble (*Alabastro a glaccione*) • Arencia • Onyx marble (*Alabastro a rosa*) • Onyx marble (*Alabastro a giaccione*) • Breccia di Susa • Onyx marble (*Alabastro giallo*) • Pavonazetto chiaro • Onyx marble • Onyx marble (*Alabastro a rosa*) • Sette Basi minuta • Granito fiorito • Onyx marble (*Alabastro a tartaruga*) • Calcite • Breccia pavonazza
CIRCLE D	Cippolino mandolato rosso • Giallo di Siena • Granito del Foro Trajano • Onyx marble • Africano nero • Onyx marble (*Alabastro a nuvole*) • Breccia traccagnina • Onyx marble (*Alabastro fiorito*) • Lumachella di Trieste • Astracane • Onyx marble (*Alabastro di Orta*) • Breccia di Susa • Onyx marble • Breccia verde d'Egitto • Onyx marble (*Alabastro a pecorella chiaro*) • Onyx marble (*Alabastro rosso*) • Cipollino mandolato verde • Onyx marble (*Alabastro di Montaulo*) • Rosso di levanto • Breccia corallina rosso • Giallo e nero di Porto Venere • Jasper (*Diaspro*) • Onyx marble (*Alabastro giallo*) • Astracane • Calcite • Onyx marble (*Alabastro rosso*) • Broccatellone • Breccia di Serravezza minuta • Breccia d'Arno • Verde di Corsica
CIRCLE E	Onyx marble (*Alabastro a giaccione*) • Porta Santa fiorita • Onyx marble (*Alabastro di Montauto*) • Perfido verde • Breccia di Serravezza • Fior di persico • Occhio di pavone • Porta Santa lionata • Onyx marble (*Alabastro a occhi*) • Porfido rosso • Lumachello di Abrozzo • Broccatello de Tortosa • Cipollio rosso • Breccia di Aleppo • Onyx marble (*Alabastro a rosa*) • Pavonazzetto • Breccia di Simone • Porfido • Giallo paglia • Onyx marble (*Alabastro pavo razzo*) • Breccia ombrata • Astracane • Africano rosso • Giallo antico • Lumachella • Paesina rossa • Onyx marble (*Alabastro a occhi*) • Sette Basi • Rosso antico • Africano fiorito

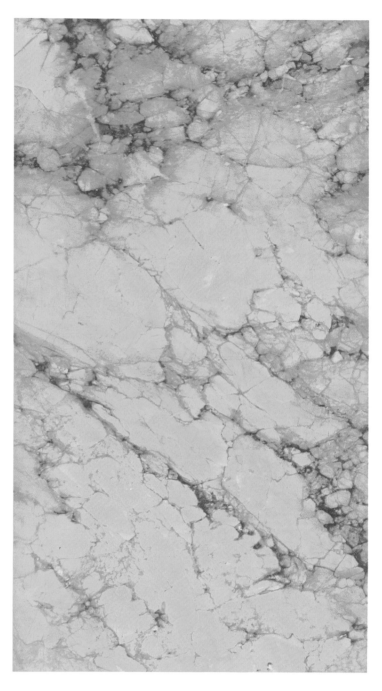

When Thomas Kershaw exhibited these fine painted panels he was accused of using real Yellow Sienna marble (see page 104).

reveal a great variety of patterns, such as the popular Serpentines, whose distinctive, green stones are evident on many building facades.

Minerals

The crystalline substances found in rocks, and in pure deposits, minerals are highly prized as decorative stones in their own right; turquoise, opal, malachite and quartz being amongst the better known examples.

Marble names

In general, the popular or commercial names of marble, as opposed to their geological classification, are derived either from a poetic description of the visual attributes of the stone, the region or country of origin, or the name of the quarry or quarry owner where the deposit is or was found. Many of the great marbles of antiquity are suffixed by the name 'antique', signifying that the stone has been mined to extinction, or the location of the source lost. However, popular demand often results in deposits being rediscovered, or an alternative source being found.

Areas of use

A brief description of the physical properties of marble will indicate those areas where it is commonly used, and thus where a painted illusion may be most profitably employed. Generally, marbles are extremely dense stones that perform well under compression, but poorly under tension. Consequently, whilst they are used as building blocks, such as in columns or slabs, they are unsuitable for bridging materials, like beams. The most popular decorative application is in the form of a cladding or facing material. The thin veneers are fragile, and often pliable, and thus must be adequately supported, or securely mounted to a firm structure. Consequently, whilst marble is often

natural translucency of skin, and it has proved a firm, if expensive, favourite with craftsmen for over two thousand years. However, there are many other beautiful variegated marbles that

applied to walls and floors, its physical limitations make it totally unsuitable for use on ceilings or overhangs. However, these limitations are only intended as a rough guide. During the course of marbling you will find that contradiction of these guidelines often can produce eye-catching results.

By way of conclusion, the importance of seeing marble at first hand cannot be over-emphasised. Visit the natural history and geological museums to look at individual stones, and take lots of photographs for future reference. To see marble 'in situ' visit prestigious buildings, such as churches, banks, stately homes, hotels and restaurants. This will show you how marble interacts with nature, other building materials and, most importantly, people.

MARBLING

Throughout history decorative painters have been commissioned by architects and designers to capture the magic of marble in paint. It is perhaps during the Renaissance that we see the clearest evidence of the marbling tradition. The designers of many grandiose schemes stipulated the use of marble in forms and situations which would have extended the natural stone far beyond its physical and practical limitations. For example, whilst double concaves could be sculpted, even in a laminate form the natural weight of the material presented insuperable problems as regards fixing, safety and maintenance. Consequently, close inspection reveals the hand of the marbler to be present in many of the intricate reliefs and domed and vaulted ceilings of buildings of the day. Often perched hundreds of feet above the ground, they literally filled in the gaps to maintain the continuity of the marble surface. Similarly, the

Romans combined the painted illusion with the natural material, despite having access to limitless quantities of decorative stone, and using it in an unreserved and flamboyant manner.

While few of us can hope to achieve such results, Kershaw's Serpentine marble (see page 114) sets a standard to aim for.

This Kershaw panel shows the ringed fossils and disjointed veining system characteristic of Belgium Red or Rouge Royale marbles (see page 124).

This style is reflected in the almost fairground atmosphere of many Greek Orthodox and Italian churches, where the technique finds expression in a crude but nevertheless effective form.

In France, on the other hand, marbling tends to be precise and rather formal. An example of this classical approach is shown on page 37 (top). And in America, marblers have preferred the bolder approach, using gaudy patterning and opaque colours to convey the effect.

It is in England that we find, perhaps, the most successful expression of the craft: in the 1850s the work of men like John Taylor and Thomas Kershaw set a standard that has not been surpassed since, and any serious student of marbling should inspect the many examples of their work in the Victoria and Albert Museum, London, and the Chadwick Museum, Bolton. Samples of Kershaw's marbling are shown here and on pages 18 and 19.

Contemporary uses

The media, whether it be film, theatre or television, exploits the illusion of marbling whenever the need arises to imply integrity, honesty or formality. Look out for the blurred diagonals in the backdrop when next viewing a party political broadcast.

Marbled surfaces are often seen in old comedy films featuring the Marx Brothers or Charlie Chaplin. The 'Establishment' image of marble creates a wonderful foil against which to contrast their irreverent, anarchic humour. Similarly, clever use of the illusion reflected the hedonistic style of the 30s, as Fred Astaire and Ginger Rogers danced their magic in countless marbled settings.

Shopping areas provide us with our most immediate example of the recent popularity of marbling. Marbling has become synonymous with a sense of awareness, and a simulation is currently 'de rigeur' in the more stylish boutiques and antique shops.

For many people today, the financial pressures of renting or buying a house mean that there is little surplus income to spend on expensive fitments around the home. The painted illusion of marbling represents a practical way of introducing colour, elegance and atmosphere into their surroundings.

Approaches to marbling

To some, marbling is an academic exercise in replication; a discipline that combines a thorough knowledge of the natural stone and the medium of paint, with a painstaking attention to detail. Whilst their work is undoubtedly impressive, over large areas it can look rather sterile and contrived, lacking something of the essential spontaneity of less formal attempts.

To others, marbling is a matter of suggesting rather than stating the illusion; of attempting to capture 'the essence' of the polished stone in paint. By essence I mean abstract qualities such as solidity, cloudiness, depth, translucency and motion (see pages 96-9). Whilst this work often bears little more than a passing reference to any particular marble, and therefore is quite aptly described as 'fantasy', the intention is for the illusion to be convincing, and not necessarily authentic.

There are many people who can marble an individual panel beautifully, but fail miserably when applying the technique as part of a decorative scheme for a domestic setting. Conversely, some of the crudest attempts at marbling may be very successful merely because they are in sympathy with their surrounding environment, and they capture the essence of the stone.

So, the formal and traditional techniques are there to be mastered, but not slavishly obeyed. Bend the rules and encourage the 'happy accident'; experiment with colour, and don't be afraid to attempt large areas or unconventional subjects. Remember, failed attempts are not terminal – a new start is only a coat of paint away.

This illustration of a Kershaw panel shows a heavily veined variety of Red Levanto (see page 106).

MARBLING IN THE HOME

This chapter examines traditional and contemporary examples of marbling for the home. It covers suitable themes and decorative schemes for every room in the house.
With a little planning, imagination and common sense you can use marbling to create the style and mood of your choice around the house. It can be employed to emphasise desirable features, adjust scale, and alleviate poor proportion.

USING THE ILLUSION

The successful incorporation of a marbled theme within the home will depend upon the accuracy with which you appraise which areas might benefit from a marbled treatment, what are the most suitable marble types for those areas, and the scale you should work to for any particular design.

Background or feature?

The visual weight and presence of a marbled surface can be accurately controlled by the combination of colour and pattern (see pages 96-9). On the one hand, opaque colour contrasts and dense patterns will produce strident finishes that may be used to highlight features; whilst pale glazes and imprecise veining will provide anonymous surfaces, against which selected artefacts may be featured.

Small objects or isolated features

If these need to be highlighted they can be given vivid treatments, using strong colours and high density patterning. However, if the pattern is in vivid contrast to the ground colour, it is advisable to reduce the density in order to avoid the piece becoming too heavy. This process is very much one of feel and experience, but if you are unsure a quick, coloured sketch will often help.

Large objects and areas

Items like fireplaces or decorative alcoves must be treated carefully. While a fireplace is obviously a feature, heavy treatments can produce an overbearing monumentality. For effective treatments see pages 38-9.

An alcove is generally used as a display area and must be treated as a backdrop. To avoid the alcove overpowering the exhibits, restraint must be exercised as the recess has a three-dimensional form, which can be over-emphasised by a too heavy or detailed treatment.

Areas such as walls and floors must be marbled in sympathy with the rest of the room and its contents. In general, small rooms can only handle large areas of marbling as a backdrop, rather than a feature. Large rooms can absorb much

A classical alcove feature based on a column and shell motif is visually strengthened by marbling the piece in a fantasy Sienna technique (see page 104). Note how the diagonal pattern in the marbling emphasises the vertical posture of the featured vase. The pale green ground constructed in a contrasting dragging technique (see page 66) serves as a subtle backdrop for the alcove, and the whole composition is effectively framed by the moulded border.

An authentic marble floor and steps are combined with a variety of marbling techniques in this light-hearted illusion. While a small marbled panel rescues an awkward corner, a simple trompe l'oeil theme, depicting squared columns in plain relief, gives the interior a classical feel.

The generous proportions of this anteroom allow a panelling scheme on the grand scale that would certainly look out of place in a more confined setting. Fantasy marbling techniques have been employed on the panels beneath the dado rail, whilst the various features of the doors and frames have been attractively picked out using a number of different marble simulations. Combined with a clouded marbled ceiling, the overall effect may be rather too rich for some tastes – but it is certainly difficult to ignore.

greater saturations of pattern and colour, and thus comfortably accommodate marbled walls or floors as features in their own right.

Using panelling systems

When used in laminate form, as a clad-ding material, marble is cut into manageable sections or panels to facilitate handling, positioning and fixing. Working within the physical limitations of the material, the architect or designer must stipulate the dimensions of these panels, and indicate their posi-

advantage when tackling more ambitious schemes.

There are two ways to create marble panels in paint: either you can paint them directly on to the prepared surface, or you can decorate hardboard panels and then attach these to the wall, floor or piece of furniture. Both systems have their advantages and disadvantages (see page 86).

When using a panel system over large areas of wall or floor the illusion of marble on the grand scale can be created. In addition, carefully constructed marbled panels may be positioned in such a way as to emphasise the vertical or horizontal accents within a room. This allows you to visually adjust the scale and proportion of the room by effectively distancing or drawing in walls, or lowering or raising the ceiling. (The design and construction of panelling systems is discussed in more detail on pages 86-93.)

The detail above illustrates quite clearly the wide variety of marbling techniques employed in this decorative scheme. The door panels are surrounded by gilded mouldings that effectively mirror the framed paintings hanging above the dado rail. The highly polished and reflective quality of the marbling on the door panels blends well with the polished floor, providing a necessary 'lightening' effect.

tion within the scheme.

Consequently, by constructing a marbled theme within clearly defined panels, not only is the appearance of authenticity conveyed, but also the surface to be marbled is broken up into manageable areas. This is a distinct

USING THEMES

Classical Themes

The historical connection between marble and the civilisations of ancient Greece and Rome provides us with a ready-made formula for expressing a classical theme.

The success of the illusion is dependent upon conveying the grandeur and sense of space created by the use of such elements as columns and colonnades, marble floors, and monumental structures and statues. The rather formal geometry of this style of architecture allows it to be readily interpreted in a simplified, yet instantly recognisable, form. Such schemes should not be undertaken without detailed planning. Designs are prepared first on graph paper, scaled up and then transcribed on to the surface to be marbled. Areas that are to receive the various paint treatments must be clearly marked out, and from that point on the work becomes a case of painting-by-numbers, on the grand scale.

Simple *trompe l'oeil* shading techniques enable you to suggest the solidity of round or square-sectioned columns. Using elementary perspective you can recreate a receding colonnade or marble floor – an illusion that can be most effective in suggesting a sense of space within a small room. Continuing a *trompe l'oeil* theme over more than one surface can produce an exciting panoramic aspect.

Once certain basic techniques have been mastered, a painted obelisk will be within the reach of most people. A good starting point might be to check out the local garden centre for a selection of classical artefacts and statues. You will find that such items are reasonably priced, easily prepared for a suitable marbling treatment (see pages 78-83) and provide an effective, three-dimensional accompaniment to a *trompe l'oeil* decorative scheme.

A modern interpretation of the classical theme currently in vogue is 'classical jazz'. This style might be described as a 'reflection of bygone splendour'. It is a romantic view of the crumbling opulence often found in grand buildings that have fallen into disuse and disrepair. Whether this is a nostalgic reference to departed quality, or a crude salute to a decadent future, it is without doubt theatrical in appearance.

The ground rules are simple: strip the room, flat or house of all but the barest essentials; hang some torn drapes at the window, and let your paint techniques do the rest. A marbled floor, dulled with age, its geometric pattern disturbed by what appears to be some ominous structural fault, sets the scene. A marbled fireplace, monumental and crumbling, supports the lone candle that illuminates the proceedings. Classical artefacts, such as pillars and busts ravaged by time, stand forlornly aloof in the gloom. . .

The paint techniques employed are a combination of antiquing (the ageing of surfaces), *trompe l'oeil* and, of course, marbling.

When marble ages, naturally its surface dulls, the colour and pattern becomes less defined and faults appear, especially at the junctions of major veins. These features may be represented in paint by tinting the final coats of clear, matt varnish, which protect the finish, with a hint of yellow-green. Also, try accentuating major veining patterns with dramatic colours or revealing some contrasting background to fractures. Another worthwhile effect is 'dislocating' adjoining panels, to suggest structural flaws in the room, and painting debris from a fractured marble panel, frieze or statue on to the marbled floor, to emphasise the impression of decay.

A 30s theme

Although the 1930s look drew its inspiration from a vibrant arts and crafts movement that had emerged around the turn of the century, it was the social climate of the day that moulded its popular image. The realities of a world in political turmoil and economic depression were ignored, in favour of a seductive cinematic fantasy. The reference point for style, elegance, taste and behaviour was the Hollywood dream. Most interiors were decorated with flat, painted surfaces which served as backdrops for the display of fashionable furniture and artefacts of the day. With the traditional association between marble and opulence, the stone provided an excellent contrast against which to feature these items. It was used extensively on walls and floors, where panels were often expressed as combinations of simple, geometric shapes, such as fans, elipses and staggered columns.

These surfaces were often painted in highly polished black, dark green and red marble, and were featured against pale, satin-faced, travertine stone. A passing reference to classicism was made with the appearance of Greek friezes and boldly stated panel framing.

In many ways this was a period of excess, a characteristic revealed by the extensive use of marble in small, intimate rooms, such as studies and bedrooms. In some cases entire walls and ceilings were panelled in one particular marble. Although the marble was generally of a subdued tone, extensive use was made of 'book end' repeat patterning (see page 89), and the over-all theme became somewhat strident and overpowering. The finish, whilst undoubtedly 30s, is very much an acquired taste. However, there are many reference books available on this period, and you will have little difficulty in finding more restrained examples for inspiration.

Abstract fantasy

An abstract expression of marble may be used to create all manner of themes. By dispensing not only with the conventional marble panelling system, but also with the geometric disciplines of the walls, floor and ceiling, we can paint marbled patterns that link these surfaces, and create illusions that throw into question the very shape of the room. Basically, dramatic effects are achieved with strident veining patterns striking out over a contrasting ground. For example, the pattern may be a pronounced diagonal that drags the eye over one surface and on to another or, alternatively, an arresting feature such as a lightning flash that snakes out in all directions.

These sorts of effects owe more than a passing reference to the gothic nightmares of a Ken Russell fantasy, and whilst they are fairly easy to produce, they are not for the faint-hearted.

A more reserved and rather elegant fantasy can be achieved by using one particular marbled finish on various unconnected surfaces within a room. However, whilst retaining the same colour and pattern throughout, adjust the scale of the design on each surface. Thus, for example, while the pattern-repeat on a small table may occur every 5 cm (2 in), on the fireplace it could repeat at 15 cm (6 in), and on a wall panel every 30 cm (12 in). This technique is useful for integrating seemingly disparate elements in a room.

ENTRANCES, HALLS, STAIRWAYS AND LANDINGS

These areas are notoriously difficult to decorate in a manner that relates to the rest of the house. They tend to be rather dowdy and, because they are heavily used areas, often reflect general wear and tear in the form of peeling wallpaper, tatty carpets and cracked plaster. Because they provide visitors with their first view of the inside of your home, and because all other rooms lead off them, and therefore they link all rooms to each other, entrances play a very important role in the decorative scheme of the house.

Usually, the problem is one of establishing continuity and character. In both instances marbled surfaces can provide successful solutions.

Continuity is achieved by using one marble type throughout. And as a rule any impression of restriction or confinement can be improved by simulating a marble with understated colour and indeterminate, random veining.

In some homes corridor areas appear disproportionately high. Ceilings can be 'lowered' by marbling a darker and heavier looking marble below waist height, and contrasting it with a lighter, painted colour above. If combined with a simple *trompe l'oeil* painted dado rail, this creates the illusion of looking over a low wall. If there is a skirting board use it to create a contrasting break with the floor surface. If

In contrast to the confined spaces characteristic of small homes, this vast hall has been rescued from mediocrity by the construction of a marbled floor. The simple pattern successfully reflects the scale of the building, while the chosen colours echo the decor of wall and ceiling to produce a coherent scheme. Although rather formal, the theme is essentially one of space and light.

This hallway cleverly incorporates marbled elements into the predominantly black and gold theme. The dark marbling on the door frame, stair riser and skirting is understated, yet of sufficient strength to imply quality and character. The theme is continued with the dark diamonds on the marbled floor establishing a flow pattern through the area. A clever counterbalance is achieved by marbling the umbrella stand in a reversed theme, white-veined marble (see page 100).

there isn't one a painted section will suffice. However, another marbled technique would appear fussy, so use a flat paint of roughly the same tone as the colour above the rail. A final refinement would be to create a *trompe l'oeil* theme above the dado rail, depicting very simple three-dimensional, abstract, marble panelling.

The passage of the stairwell, from one level to another, presents us with one of the most visually dramatic and practically challenging features in the home. Decorating it is usually a balancing act on ladders, with little opportunity to step back and view progress. However, the hard work can be very rewarding. It is a good idea to continue with the same marble theme on the walls as in the hall, but lightening it as it approaches a white ceiling. This gives a pleasing impression of light from above; particularly useful in a gloomy area. Hand rails and spindles

Although the Breche Pernise marble used for this hall is densely patterned and strong in colour saturation, the translucency of its surface prevents the effect from becoming overbearing. Lightly marbled door frames echo the colour of the support beams and unadorned columns provide a natural contrast to the busy patterns on wall and ceiling.

The architectural features of a curved staircase right, are strengthened by marbling treads and risers in a lightly contrasting yellow fantasy. The vertical spindles and diagonal floor pattern provide interesting foils to the technique.

are best left as contrasts, in flat paint. Unless of course, they are to be a theme in their own right. For example, solid handrail supports can be given a simple geometric *trompe l'oeil* treatment, depicting a marbled balustrade. But do remember that detailed treatments of inaccessible or heavily contoured items, such as spindles or relief work in plaster, can be a repetitive chore, especially if the latter are situated high up.

Marbling floors is a highly effective method of providing continuity between the hall and rooms leading off it. Patterns constructed on the diagonal are particularly successful in implying directional flow. Floors are less obtrusive than walls, and therefore can be given much bolder treatments. Deciding upon a pattern repeat is very much

Continuity, flow and character have been dramatically enhanced in this narrow hallway by creating a marbled fantasy throughout. The predominantly white theme, which is continued in the floor tiling, reflects the available light and prevents the space from becoming claustrophobic.

protect against scuffing.

A slightly less ambitious scheme is to create a visual link between all the doors leading off a hall or landing. As subjects for marbling, doors provide a good introduction to the technique. Unlike floors, they are small enough to be tackled in a day and, if the frame is picked out from the panels, they allow a combination of two or more techniques to be tried out and contrasted with each other. The doors can be decorated with similar or contrasting marble types, as just the suggestion of marble will be strong enough to establish the link between them. A continuous *trompe l'oeil* dado rail linking the doors can be used to reinforce the sense of continuity.

As we know, in reality a marble door would be a practical impossiblility. Consequently, marbling one is no more than a fantasy interpretation, and therefore there are no restrictions on how it should look. This is a perfect opportunity to experiment with the ways in which the painted illusion can suggest varying degrees of weight and formality. Try pale colours and understated patterns to produce a rather pleasing lightweight effect; or employ heavy contrasts, and explicit veining on the diagonal, to produce a more dramatic look – especially if the door frame is incorporated in the finish. On flat-faced doors, *trompe l'oeil* shading effects can be constructed around marbled sections, to suggest relief panels. Alternatively, a similar effect may be achieved by constructing borders, using a contrasting marbled technique, or flat paint.

Halls, stairs and landings are busy spaces, so don't waste time on too much detail. People pass through rather than dwell in these areas; it is the grand effect that will carry the day.

a matter of seeing if it looks right 'in situ'. You will find a paper diagram, to scale, of the plan usually suggests the correct balance. Always put in a contrasting border around a patterned floor, even if it is only in flat paint. This will provide a clean break from the wall, and accommodate irregularities in the geometry of the building, or your technique. Apply several protective coats of clear polyurethane finish, to

THE LIVING AREA

In a family home, communal areas such as living rooms tend to reflect the personality of the group, rather than any one individual. Comfortable old furniture, cherished memorabilia and dusty shelves, cluttered with photographs and books, are all part of a reassuring disorder. It is the people and their possessions which provide the atmosphere. Consequently, any decorative treatment other than a softly stated backdrop would be an intrusion.

In these circumstances, the efforts of the aspiring decorative painter are best directed to recycling pieces of furniture.

The scuffed coffee table, the anonymous chest and the old piano are just a coat of paint away from becoming prized objets d'art. For decorative and practical advice on marbling furniture see pages 50-2, 82-3 and 93.

For those with fewer family commitments, the living room is subjected to far less wear and tear. It becomes not only a place to relax, but also a slightly more formal area in which to entertain visitors and friends. In this case the decor can be far more personalised and expressive. A carefully chosen marbling theme can clearly reflect your

Right: In this elegant, spacious interior marbling has been used extensively on both large wall areas and detailed relief work alike. Natural room proportions and openings have been framed and strengthened in contrasting techniques, and continuity has been established by echoing the theme from one room to the next. The highly polished parquet floor provides a pleasing foil and underscores the quality of the interior.

A mottled blue fantasy marbling technique has been incorporated within a simple trompe l'oeil *theme to establish a classical perspective. The skirting board in painted relief is echoed in the cornice. Disregard of the natural arch has produced a peculiar visual tension within the composition.*

No fewer than five contrasting marbling techniques have been used to create this beautiful panelling system. Note how the darker technique that establishes the horizontal definition at dado rail and skirting height is continued on to the door frame to strengthen the opening.

A trompe l'oeil *theme has been used to establish a classical feel within this elegant dining/living room. Marbled columns, ballustrades and friezes frame the cloud formations, providing the occupants of the room with an almost heavenly perspective on life. The airy feel is accentuated by good natural light, with the marbled sections clearly identified, yet unobtrusively stated, in a reserved, white-veined fantasy (see page 124).*

personal preferences for atmosphere, mood and style.

A living room is probably the best area to try out themes (see pages 28-9). A common approach is to marble the fireplace, window frame, picture and dado rail and skirting board in a single, often overstated, technique. Whilst this acts as a cohesive factor for the room, strong horizontal accents do tend to visually lower the ceiling, and this is not necessarily a desirable effect. Also, marbling thin sections of timber, such as skirtings and picture rails, in high relief can look unconvincing.

Decoratively, marble is at its most successful as a flat, uninterrupted surface, offset or bordered by natural breaks, such as skirtings or coving, decorated in a flat paint.

Visually, the walls are the most important surfaces in the room. Any large-scale marbling scheme should be preceded by careful planning of the various simulations and panel locations. Before you start, it is essential to have a clear idea in mind of the intended strength or presence of the overall finish and its relationship to the rest of the room.

In this classically-inspired room the skirting board and dado rail have been picked out in a darker marble simulation. Had the opposite been attempted, with dark wall panels and lighter skirting, the room could have appeared top-heavy and unbalanced. As it is, the room provides a superb setting for all the real and simulated marble furnishings.

Light-coloured marbling can bring a fresh, spacious, airy feel to a room. Note too how well this light grey marbling contrasts with the dark wood table.

As a general rule, it is better to understate the marbling. It is quite easy to make the finish too heavy for the room, and it is far easier to strengthen an illusion than to tone it down.

Another important point to take into consideration at the planning stage is that where two marbling techniques meet on the horizontal, say at the junction of a picture or dado rail, you should ensure that the darker simulation is nearest to the floor. If the converse is tried, the room will appear top heavy and unbalanced.

Marbled floors are dealt with in detail on pages 91-3. As part of a decorative scheme they are generally represented by a simple, geometric repeat that, in terms of scale and pattern, is in proportion and in keeping with the rest of the room. They can be used as a feature in their own right, although do remember that large items of furniture may well conceal some of the pattern. Furniture that stands off the floor, on legs, will be less intrusive.

FIREPLACES

Most living rooms have a fireplace, and the elegant English, French and Italian fireplaces of the eighteenth century have conveyed a sense of authority and opulence to the interiors in which they have been incorporated. Consequently, whilst they have always been in great demand, today the steep price tag for a reasonable example adds a certain incentive when attempting the painted illusion.

Other than as a source of heat, fireplaces are employed primarily as a focal point for a room, and as such are designed to be in proportion to the scale of their surroundings. Consequently, it is important to control your use of a marbling technique, in order to prevent the illusion from becoming monumental and overstated. White-veined marble (see page 100), with a hint of powdered colour and a loosely described pattern, is a safe bet.

Various looks can be achieved by simple changes of technique. For example, by picking-out the various components of the fire with slight variations in tone and line, the formal geometry and elegance of the piece will be emphasised. On the other hand, the use of patchy, contrasting colours and random veining, which ignore the structural elements of the piece, will dissolve the visual form and imply an abstract solidity. This ploy is often used to strengthen rather mean-looking fireplaces, or those represented by little more than a hole in the wall.

In the case of the latter, contrasting parallel borders, constructed around the mouth of the fire, will emphasise the structure and strengthen the appearance of solidity. A marbled hearth extending into the room underpins the effect.

For those who require an authentic fireplace, without the cost, excellent fibreglass replicas are widely available in a range of styles. Given a detailed treatment, they can be made visually indistinguishable from the real thing.

Finally, for the DIY enthusiast, a most effective contemporary theme can be achieved by constructing a simple fire surround using square or round sectioned metal ducting (available from heating and ventilation suppliers). The sections are inexpensive, and after marbling may be combined in any number of forms to create an original, contemporary feature.

Below: Not every home is blessed with an ornate fireplace; however, with thoughtful marbling even the most humble examples can be strengthened and transformed into pleasing architectural features. Here simple sponging and veining techniques have been used to identify the separate components of the surround without sacrificing the essential characteristics of its Georgian origins.

Far left: The return to uncluttered neo-classicism seen in this early Regency fire surround is admirably complemented by thoughtful marbling. The treatment is understated and the piece, only lightly contrasted against the wall colouring, is allowed to speak for itself. A panelling system continued in a sympathetic technique below the height of the dado rail echoes the formal proportions of the fireplace and its relationship to the scale of the room.

Top left: Although the marbler has concentrated on featuring this elegant piece in one type of marble, the individual components of the fire surround are clearly identified by using the directional flow of the veining system to contrast adjacent sections. The framed and featured marbled panels above reinforce the classical proportions of the piece.

Left: A real marble fireplace is beautifully set off by the use of light-coloured, symetrically positioned marbled panels. The panelling also complements the chairs which are placed either side of the fireplace. The overall effect is one of elegant proportion and harmony.

THE BEDROOM

Bedrooms are not only a place to sleep, but also somewhere to study and relax. They are private and intimate areas; retreats from the hustle and bustle of the outside world. Consequently, the decor tends to be highly personalised, reflecting the aspirations and fantasies of the occupants.

Bedrooms are usually dominated by the size and position of the furniture, with the bed almost always providing a natural focal point, and the inspiration for the rest of the decor. For example, a traditional theme involves marbling the bedhead and skirting board with a matching technique, and continuing the treatment on doors, window frames and bedside tables. As an added refinement, the latter may be marbled and then decorated with reflective inlay

Right: This simple yet effective treatment demonstrates the strength of marbling as an illusion. A humble melamine bedhead is transformed into a slab of polished marble. A marbled bedside chest and plant pot extend the fantasy.

Far right (top): Although crude, this horizontally displayed panel incorporates an unmistakable signature – a mottled, cloudy ground and a fractured diagonal vein. Marble is implied; the object being to echo the colours of the drapes, and possibly the garden beyond, rather than replicate a specific marble.

Far right (bottom): Doors and door frames are a popular choice for a fantasy marbled theme. In this instance, even the fine elements of the window frame have been incorporated in a tongue-in-cheek illusion. The technique has been extended along the adjacent wall surfaces, skirting board and fitted cupboards to establish continuity in a restricted space. Once again the dado rail is used to provide a natural panel break.

work, using iridescent shell and metallic foil. This effect can be extended to the bedhead.

Similarly, wardrobes, dressing tables, vanity units and bed supports can be marbled as features in their own right, and offset by using flat paint on the walls. Conversely they may be used to complement marbled panels applied to the walls, floors or even ceilings.

Marbled floor designs should take into account the position of permanent items of furniture, such as the bed. There is little point in working out a fascinating pattern repeat merely to have most of it obscured.

Marbled walls that are intended to be features in their own right can take fairly strong colours and heavy veining. However, you should avoid sharp contrasts between the walls and the floor, as the atmosphere should be restful. The general idea is that the eye is gently led, rather than forcefully directed over the marbled surface. The exception to this rule is the ever popular black and gold marble (see page 102), in which yellow veins hang like a linked chain against a glassy, black ground. The pattern is strident, but the overall effect is of tasteful formality.

Because a considerable amount of time is spent reclining in the bedroom, the upper sections of the room are rewarding areas to marble. Marbled friezes are particularly effective, and ceiling roses and light fittings can be used to generate a simple geometric pattern, which can be carried out in contrasting marble techniques. However, it is better to work the contrasting techniques horizontally on panel sections (see pages 84-93), and then subsequently secure them to the ceiling. To do this, either locate the joists and fix the panels on with screws or use strong adhesive over the panel back.

THE BATHROOM

Although the bathroom is the most private area in the home, and its function specifically defined, it is employed in a number of ways and therefore must be flexible in use. On some occasions it is little more than a utilitarian box; a place to take a swift shower or have a shave. At other times it ought to be a luxurious temple; a place to wash off the grime and stress of the day; a place of relaxation and contemplation. These factors must be taken into account when planning a scheme.

Whether you choose a classical scheme, or something a little more 'avant garde', usually the bathroom suite is treated as a neutral foil against which to contrast a marble theme, and traditionally the bath and basin surrounds, the skirting board and the door and window frames are marbled in the same technique. The alternative approach is to continue a floor design up the side of the bath surround and on to the adjacent walls, taking it up to about shoulder height.

However, a more effective method is to marble the walls in a mid-tone, with a delicate, loose but uniformly patterned veining system. This gives a finish that looks a bit like an intricate road map. Surfaces marbled in this manner provide a restful fantasy of dramatic landscapes, half-recognised faces and mythological beasts. While the effect will visually close in what is

Right: The generous proportions of the bathroom have allowed the marbler free range to construct this blue fantasy on both walls and ceiling. The insistent patterning and sharp contrast of the superimposed veins might well have proved too oppressive in a more confined space.

This unusual treatment of a bathroom gives some indication of the boundless possibilities open to the imaginative decorator. The traditional French vitreous enamelled bath has been marbled in subdued tones. Although centrally positioned as a feature, it is not intended to compete with the heavily patterned walls.

Mirrors can be used to suggest space in restricted areas. In this instance there is an added bonus, a clever bookend pattern motif (see page 89) has been achieved using the reflection of the marbled panel in the bathroom mirror. Norwegian Breche Rose is the featured marble.

usually a small room, this is not necessarily a bad thing. The womb-like atmosphere can be psychologically reassuring if you contemplate the world whilst lying in the bath.

It is advisable to compensate for any disproportionately high ceilings with wall-mounted, strategically placed mirrors. These will provide an illusion of lateral space. A similar effect may be achieved by introducing a low, artificial light source, such as a wall light with a marbled shade. Alternatively, a hanging basket positioned high up in the room will distract the eye – plants thrive in the warm, moist atmosphere of a bathroom and are a very effective complement to marbled surfaces.

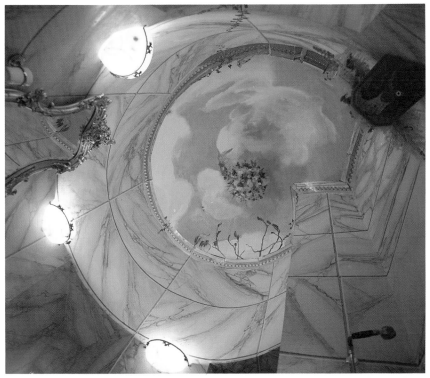

To relieve any claustrophobic feeling in this confined circular room, the artist has effectively taken the roof off the building by painting a trompe l'oeil scene on the ceiling. Artificial light substitutes for natural daylight, illuminating the translucent marbled finish.

Far left: A powerful marbling technique has been used in this bathroom setting to create an eye-catching feature. The marbler has disregarded the panelled structure of the fitted unit and, by marbling the horizontal surface and adjacent wall, has produced an illusion of great solidity and formality.

For the more adventurous, such a decorative scheme can be turned on its head. Namely, the bathroom suite could be marbled as a feature in its own right, and the other surfaces decorated with flat paint to provide the contrast. (Though in more spacious bathrooms it is possible to encompass all surfaces with a marbling treatment.) This

Left: Although the pattern is insistent, the flowing qualities of the veining keep the eye moving over the surfaces, and in so doing imply space. The fitted shelves, marbled in a similar manner, have a certain sculptural quality.

The formal panel system has been abandoned in this dramatic fantasy as contrasting veins strike out diagonally over the entire mottled wall surface. Although the veins are visually prominent, they are sparsely displayed so that the marbled finish provides a neutral backdrop to the bathroom furniture.

A dramatic marbling technique is used in this bathroom setting. The formal panelled structure of the fitted cupboard is disregarded as the bold veining strikes out in all directions over a mottled ground. The illusion of formality and solidity is further enhanced by continuing the pattern onto an adjacent wall.

approach has been made possible with the development of epoxy-based paints for repairing or rejuvenating ceramic and enamelled surfaces. Whilst these paints are available in only a limited range of colours, they open up a whole range of decorative possibilities. But it should be noted that whilst the inside of the bath and basin may be marbled, only the outside, and not the inside, of the lavatory pan is recommended for treatment. And you must bear in mind that any treatment of the bathroom suite will render it out of commission for a few days.

Bathrooms tend to suffer from inadequate natural light, and in these circumstances, whilst the use of blues and greens undoubtedly reflects the feeling of water, when applied over large areas their effect can be quite chilling. The introduction of yellow-red pastels, opaque ochres or mauvey-beiges can visually warm the atmosphere. Whatever colours you choose, bear in mind that there is a lot of water about, so all treated surfaces must be carefully sealed with varnish in order to protect them against the penetration of moisture.

THE KITCHEN

Nowadays the kitchen is a busy place that often doubles-up as a second dining area. Usually, it is a collection of storage units, appliances, pots and pans and all manner of food packets and electronic gadgetry. In these circumstances, marbled wall and work surfaces should not attempt to compete. They should be treated as an anonymous backdrop to the jangle of equipment and activity.

Despite being on a horizontal plane, work surfaces and table tops are visually prominent, so care should be taken in the choice and strength of colour. Although a white-vein marble technique is always a safe bet (see page 100), a softly stated pastel, which contrasts with units above and below the work surface, can provide an attractive finish. Work surfaces that have been marbled, and will be subjected to heavy use, should be protected with something more substantial than polyurethane varnish. Transparent epoxy or polyester resins will work well. However, they do tend to leave a sweet smell that lingers until they have fully cured. Unless you are fully conversant with these materials, employ them on a trial surface before starting in earnest on the worktop.

The doors of storage units are ideal surfaces to marble. Being situated above and below natural eye level, they can be given quite bold treatments. There is the added advantage that doors can be removed one at a time, and marbled on the horizontal. Melamine is a good surface to work on, and

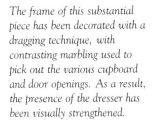

The frame of this substantial piece has been decorated with a dragging technique, with contrasting marbling used to pick out the various cupboard and door openings. As a result, the presence of the dresser has been visually strengthened.

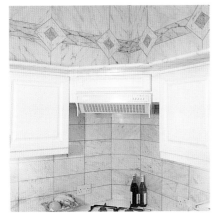

requires a minimal amount of preparation (see pages 76-83). A marbled dining table, in a matching technique, gives a pleasant appearance and ties together horizontal and vertical surfaces.

Kitchen floors tend to be heavily used. So, whilst a painted surface has much to recommend it in terms of ease of cleaning, a detailed marbled pattern would be lost under foot. It is best to opt for bold, panelled contrasts, and to seal the finish with several coats of varnish, to protect it against moisture and heavy traffic. Alternatively, consider using specially formulated floor paints.

You will find that various appliances, such as the refrigerator, washing machine and stove, are particularly appropriate subjects for fantasy marbling. Their smooth, hard surfaces provide an excellent ground on which to marble, and a bold technique can imply a monumental presence. This tongue-in-cheek approach can be emphasised by using a *trompe l'oeil* scene, depicting the contents of the chosen appliance – marbled of course.

Fantasy effect (left)
This peach fantasy marble has a strong diagonal that is carried through from the drawer to the unit and wall cupboard, giving a cohesive look.

Below: Marbling is used as a means to an end rather than an end in its own right. In this instance there is little pretence towards authenticity, marble is merely implied. The concerns of the designer are two-fold: to construct a panel that may be used as a backdrop rather than a featured surface, and to select paints that will compliment the overall colour scheme.

Formal panels (left and above)
A simple frieze provides a pleasing contrast to the white units. Positioned above eye level, it does not have to compete with the visual energy of a busy kitchen. The traditional design is constructed from contrasting marbled sections. The red central diamond is reinforced by the veining patterns in the surrounding white-veined marble (see page 100). Double book-end patterning (see page 89) reinforces the angularity of the diamonds.

FURNITURE AND ARTEFACTS

As a rule, objects that are to be marbled are treated as features in their own right, with the surrounding area providing a visual backdrop. Consequently, any technique used must be restrained to prevent large items, such as pieces of furniture, becoming overbearing, and to allow smaller, delicate pieces to retain their elegance. The visual presence of any piece can be controlled by adjusting the colour saturation and pattern density of the finish (see pages 96-9).

When items of furniture have a distinctive structure, such as chests of drawers, the use of contrasting marbling techniques or flat, painted colour on the surrounding walls and floors will provide a neutral frame to highlight the

piece. The contrast will strengthen the form of the subject, and consequently allow a more subtle finish to be used.

On the other hand, you could ignore the structure of a particular item, and continue a pattern over the different elements within it, and even over surrounding surfaces. This will destroy the form and give the piece an abstract monumentality.

The conventional rules governing the correct use of marbling, established in the latter part of the nineteenth century, deemed it 'poor taste' to marble any surface or object that could not have been made of the real material. While standards change, it is important to realise that it is difficult to suggest the presence of authentic marble

Marbling a small piece of furniture will provide you with an opportunity not only to create an eye-catching feature but also to develop paint techniques in greater detail. Much thought and effort has gone into designing this disarmingly simple, elegant and practical motif. The marbler has both created a chess-board and reflected the colour and format of the panelled floor, establishing a visual link of lasting interest. Note the delicate, swirling inlay work surrounding the rectilinear pattern, and the spattering technique carried out on the legs and side frame.

Far left: This scheme demonstrates how it is possible to incorporate a number of marbling techniques together without the effect becoming strident or overbearing. The table is treated with a strong Sienna fantasy, while the formal proportions of the fireplace require only the slightest hint of a veining pattern to imply marble. The darker tiles, the authentic material, tend to reinforce the illusion.

*The marbler has transformed
this small chest of drawers,
converting it from a lifeless,
insignificant piece of furniture
into a cherished objet d'art.
The yellow sienna fantasy has
enhanced its visual strength.
The effect has been exaggerated
by disregarding the formal
structure of drawers and frame
and continuing the technique
over all surfaces.*

unless such subjects or surfaces are chosen. For example, while a large table with a substantial base may be marbled in such a way as to imply authenticity, a delicate coffee table, no matter how clever the technique, can only be regarded as a light-hearted fantasy. Similarly, marbled objects such as televisions, hi-fi speakers or telephones pretend to be nothing more than visual jokes. We must take them for what they are, enjoy them and use them as valid contemporary design projects in appropriate settings.

The preparation of the various sur-faces that you will encounter is detailed in Chapter Five. However, there a few basic tips worth following when marbling furniture and small objects: if the object is movable, prepare it off-site, in the garage or outhouse; if not, take precautions against paint spillage and inquisitive fingers. If possible, raise the object off the floor on to a work surface, as it is easier to work on the horizontal. Where detailed inlay or panel work is required, work from sketches. And finally, once your marble effect is completely dry, you should always apply sufficient coats of protective varnish.

OUTSIDE THE HOME

The greenhouse and the garden provide a number of settings where marbled objects may be featured to good effect. Flowers and vegetation are a perfect, contrasting backdrop to the illusion.

Any object that will not drastically deteriorate when exposed to the elements may be marbled and positioned outdoors, provided the finish is protected with coats of varnish or resin.

Garden centres sell a large range of inexpensive decorative items made from plaster, stone and fibreglass, and if suitably prepared (see pages 76-83) they may all be enhanced with a painted marble effect.

An ornamental rock pool is a practical and relatively inexpensive small-scale project. Large, smooth rocks can be marbled in a range of techniques. Suitably sealed they prove a delightful foil for water, plants and of course fish. The pool itself is available as a contoured, glass fibre moulding. A marble finish implies solidity, and leaves the observer with the impression that the pool is solid rock.

Classical themes are always popular. Statues or obelisks, glimpsed through the vegetation, lend an opulent and mysterious air to a garden. Antiquing the item (see page 28), and positioning it in an overgrown thicket, will evoke an atmosphere of departed quality and neglect. In a similar vein, plastic drain-pipes and expanded foam are materials that are easily cut, prepared and marbled. They can be used as props to suggest the ruined pillars and stones of some vanished civilisation.

Various fantasy themes, which involve placing marbled icons in the alien surroundings of a garden, can be visually arresting and surrealistic, especially if their colours are in stark contrast to the surrounding vegetation. For example, a chest or trunk, part of a scrapped automobile or a truncated fibreglass column emerging from a smooth lawn at an odd angle can be both enigmatic and humorous.

Finally, whatever theme or object you choose, don't waste time on detailed simulations, unless they are to be viewed at close quarters. And make sure that you seal objects well to protect them from the elements. But bear in mind that clear coats of varnish will almost inevitably yellow with age quite quickly outdoors.

This marbled urn might be used inside or outside the home. If used outdoors, perhaps to adorn a pergola, the finish should, of course, be properly sealed against the elements using a suitable resin or varnish.

COLOUR, PAINT AND GLAZES

Traditionally, paint has provided the most practical medium for the decorative embellishment of man's environment. And its basic formula – namely, a ground pigment suspended in a transparent medium – has remained virtually unchanged for 20,000 years. The pigment, whether it be a naturally occurring organic compound or a man-made synthetic product, provides colour; the medium, whether oil, water or polymer resin based, binds that colour to a surface.

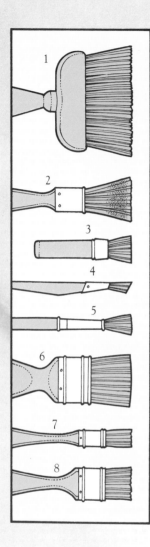

1 *Hog's hair softening brush (medium).*
2 *Hog's hair softening brush (small).*
3 *Stencil brush.*
4 *Lining fitch.*
5 *Fitch brush.*
6 *Varnishing brush.*
7 *2.5 cm (1 in) standard brush.*
8 *4 cm (1½ in) standard brush.*

Before we look at the various qualities of paints and glazes, it is worth noting that although the leading paint companies offer a comprehensive range of products, the requirements of the decorative painter are usually best served by specialist firms that stock custom colours, tinters, glazes and special brushes. If there isn't such a supplier in your locality, you can use a mail order facility (see page 128).

Always choose the best quality paint you can afford, and ask for trade formulations as they are far superior to their retail counterparts. Many specialist products come complete with a specification and instruction leaflet. These advise on such matters as recommended drying times, solvents and undercoats. Follow the advice; they want you to get the best out of their product and to be satisfied with the final result.

PAINT
Water-based and oil-based paints are the most popular types for use in domestic interiors. If you plan to use such paints in a project stick to one sort only – when in a fluid state the two systems should never be mixed. These paints are now available in thixotropic formulation, to make them non-drip. In this form they may be used for opaque ground coats, but are unsuitable for use in the preparation of coloured glazes or washes, where substantial thinning is required.

Water-based paints
These are known as emulsions or latex paints, and are available in matt, midsheen and gloss finishes as matt emulsion, vinyl silk and vinyl enamel. They may be thinned as directed by adding water, and may be applied with brush or roller to any surface other than bare

metal – which would be induced to rust. Gloss surfaces must first be rubbed down with abrasive paper, to provide a key for the paint.

They have two main advantages. Firstly, they give off little smell, and secondly they have extremely fast drying times, especially if thin coats are applied over matt emulsion (latex) grounds in a warm, dry atmosphere. However, in decorative painting it is often an advantage to lengthen the drying time, because whilst the paint remains wet, or 'alive', it can be worked and re-worked to produce the required effect. To achieve this either apply the paint over an oil-based ground, such as undercoat or eggshell; or add a small amount of glycerine (one teaspoon to one litre or two pints of thinned paint); or lower the temperature and/or increase the humidity in the room.

Matt or vinyl silk emulsions (latex paints) provide satisfactory ground coats for oil- or water-based paints, but because their finishes are unsuitable for sanding, it is impossible to get a completely smooth surface if they are used as top coats.

Although most decorators' stores now provide a mixing facility for preparing one-off colours, you can easily tint light colours yourself by adding artists' gouache to white emulsion. Gouache colour is available from specialist or art suppliers in a comprehensive range of colours, and comes in a tube or jar as a high-quality, pure pigment. It has a similar appearance to, and is compatible with, matt emulsion (latex) paint. Although it is expensive, where high-quality, accurately matched colours are required, gouache always will provide a superior finish to the ready-coloured retail emulsion (latex) paints.

Oil-based paints

These are available in matt, mid-sheen or gloss finishes, as undercoat, eggshell and gloss. They give off a pungent odour and are thinned with white (mineral) spirit. They may be painted on any finish other than whitewash or distemper. Undercoat may be applied with a brush or roller; whereas eggshell and gloss top coats are best applied with a brush on top of an undercoat.

The paints dry by a combination of chemical reaction and air drying. Thinned coats dry rapidly, but heavy gloss coats can take days to fully cure. If necessary, the drying rate can be slowed down by adding small quantities of linseed oil, or speeded up by the addition of 'liquid dryers'.

As with emulsions (latex paints), decorators' stores offer a mixing facility for oil-based paints. However, if the required shade proves elusive, custom colours are readily obtained by tinting white or pale-coloured undercoat or eggshell with artists' oils. A wide range of colours is readily available from specialist shops, in the form of concentrated pigment. Combined with white (mineral) spirit these colours produce high-quality paints in their own right. You will find that the colours produced by artists' oils are more vibrant than the ready-mixed colours of retail paints.

As an alternative to gouache or artists' oils, both the oil- and water-based systems may be be tinted with universal stainers. Although they are cheaper than artists' paints, the colour range is limited and the finish tends to be harder and less vibrant.

Acrylic paints

These bridge the gap between the oil- and water-based systems, and are available from artists' shops and specialist suppliers. Although they are thinned with water, a polymer binder is used to support the pigment. They are capable of producing a range of finishes commonly associated with both the oil- and water-based systems. For example, by adding acrylic matt medium to a thinned glaze (see page 58), the surface will reflect the ethereal quality of water-borne colour. Whereas, in contrast, the addition of an acrylic gel medium to a thinned glaze will allow the surface to reflect the juicy impasto of a Renaissance oil painting.

Acrylics have one major advantage over water-based colour: once the surface has hardened it is totally impervious to the effect of a superimposed water-based glaze. Consequently, smudged finishes are avoided. However, there is a drawback: acrylic paint must be kept mobile on the palette, or it will harden very quickly; though a drying retarder is available to slightly increase the curing time.

Although the fast drying rate of acrylics limits their flexibility, many marbling techniques may be accomplished by swift overlays of colour. For techniques where this is the case, acrylic types have a great advantage over the slower drying oil-based paints.

GLAZES AND WASHES

For our purposes the definition of a glaze is the name given to any paint that has been thinned sufficiently in order to produce a degree of transparency in the colour. And a wash is the name given to any paint that has been so substantially thinned that it leaves merely a trace of colour when applied to a surface. By changing the quantities of thinner, and thus varying the transparency of a glaze or wash, it is possible to effect quite subtle variations in both the appearance and effect of the underlying colour.

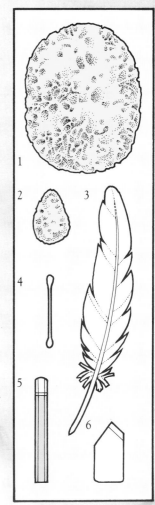

1 *Natural marine sponge.*
2 *Small piece of sponge (for cissing).*
3 *Goose feather.*
4 *Cotton bud (Q-tip).*
5 *Oil-based crayon.*
6 *Pencil eraser.*

If a wash is to be applied over an oil-based ground add one teaspoon of liquid detergent per litre (two pints) of wash.

Water-based glazes and washes

A matt or mid-sheen emulsion (latex) glaze is prepared by thinning emulsion (latex) paint with water; to a ratio of approximately one part paint to two or three parts water, depending on the degree of transparency required, and the strength and quality of the pigment in the paint.

An emulsion (latex) wash may be prepared by thinning the paint to a ratio of one part paint to as many as eight parts water. Again, the exact quantities will depend on the degree of transparency required, and the strength and quality of the pigment.

Similarly, gouache and acrylic colours may be blended with water, to produce a glaze of the required transparency. With the addition of greater quantities of water they can also be used to prepare a wash. However, a small quantity of white emulsion (latex) – one tablespoon to one litre (two pints) of prepared wash – must be added to provide 'body'.

Suitable grounds for water-based glazes and washes

Matt or mid-sheen oil- or water-based paints provide suitable grounds on which to apply water-based glazes. The ground must be smooth and hard, and oil-based ones should be lightly abraded, to provide a key for the glaze. However, emulsion (latex) grounds do tend to be quite absorbent, causing the glaze to dry quite quickly. So, if you are working on a large area and some time is needed to work the glaze, it is advisable to use an oil-based ground.

If a wash is to be applied over large areas of matt emulsion (latex), it must be carried out swiftly, with a large brush. The paint dries almost immediately, and it is very difficult to keep a wet edge. Silk emulsion (latex) grounds are less absorbent.

If a wash is to be applied over an oil-based ground, particularly eggshell finish, small quantities of liquid detergent must be added to the wash – one teaspoon per litre (two pints). The object is to break down the surface tension of the wash, and in doing so prevent it from coalescing into droplets on the surface. Abrading the ground coat with fine grade wet and dry paper (silicon carbide) will also ease the problem of a coalescing wash.

Oil-based glazes and washes

Transparent oil glaze, flatting oil or 'scumble' is available in cans from most decorating stores, as a viscous, honey-coloured or white liquid. When thinned with white (mineral) spirit and painted out, it becomes colourless. It can be used neat, but usually it is thinned with white (mineral) spirit, to a ratio of one part scumble glaze to one or two parts spirit, depending on the consistency required. The more it is thinned the faster it will 'set-up', or dry. However, scumble is not designed to be overthinned, and therefore is unsuitable for the preparation of oil-based washes.

Scumble glaze is tinted to the required colour using either artists' oils or universal stainers. It is designed to stay workable for a long time, and exhibits what are known as 'stand-up' qualities; that is, the coloured pigment held in the glaze stays put.

Thinned paint glaze is an undercoat or eggshell, oil-based paint, usually white, that is tinted with oil-based colour and thinned with white (mineral) spirit to achieve the required transparency. Because it already contains coloured pigment it is never as transparent or vibrant as tinted scumble glaze, and because it dries quickly it is more difficult to work with than scumble. Adding one teaspoon of boiled linseed oil to half a litre (one pint) of glaze will lengthen the drying time. Thinned paint glaze is readily tinted with artists' oils or universal stainers to obtain the required colour.

An oil-based wash can be created by thinning tinted, oil-based paint with white (mineral) spirit, in a ratio of one part paint to five to eight parts spirit, depending on the strength and quality of the paint pigment.

Home-made glaze, or 'gilp', is made by mixing one part boiled linseed oil with one to two parts pure turpentine, plus one part liquid drier. A teaspoon of whiting to one litre (two pints) of glaze will give it a little body. Because of the high oil content, drying can take as long as two days and the surface will always have a slight sheen. The gilp is readily tinted using artists' oils or universal tinters.

Artists' oils can be blended with white (mineral) spirit to produce excellent glazes and washes in their own right. They are expensive, and on a practical level their use is restricted to small-sized projects. They may be combined with boiled linseed oil or liquid dryers, to speed up or slow down the drying rate.

Suitable ground coats for oil-based glazes and washes

Because emulsion (latex) ground coats are unsuitable for sanding, their surfaces are invariably quite rough. Consequently, they tend to prevent an oil-based glaze from being smoothly moved over the surface; that is, they tend to 'choke' the glaze.

The ideal smooth, hard, flat surface is provided by an eggshell ground that has been rubbed flat with fine grade wet and dry paper.

Tinting glazes and washes

As we have seen, oil-based glazes and washes can be tinted with artists' oils or universal stainers, and water-based glazes and washes can be tinted with gouache or acrylic colour. In order to achieve a uniform colouring in the mix, it is advisable to use the following procedure. First place some of the tinter in a clean container. Then add a small quantity of the required solvent (white/mineral spirit for artists' oils and water for gouache), and blend thoroughly to achieve a uniformly creamy consistency. Next, add a small quantity of the glaze that is to be tinted to the mixture, and again blend thoroughly. Slowly add this mixture to your glaze, stirring all the time, until you have achieved the desired colour – test it at intervals by painting out the glaze on to paper. You will find that the stainers are very powerful, and that you need only small amounts to create the required colour.

Alternatively, when preparing a coloured glaze from a neat, white paint such as matt emulsion (latex) or undercoat, place a sufficient quantity of neat paint for the job in a container, dissolve the required tinter in the correct solvent (white/mineral spirit or water), and slowly blend it into the paint, stirring continually, until you have achieved the desired colour. The glaze is then prepared by adding the correct solvent to this mixture, to achieve the required transparency.

If you are marbling small areas, or detailing finishes, glazes can be prepared on the palette, using a brush or knife to blend the ingredients. Dippers (small containers attached to the palette), carry the necessary solvents and mediums, and these are transferred on to the palette using clean brushes.

Always be systematic about the

Tinting procedure

1 Place some of the tinter in a container. Add a small quantity of the required solvent and mix thoroughly. Add a small quantity of the glaze that is to be tinted to the mixture. Again blend thoroughly.

2 Slowly add this mixture to your glaze, stirring all the time, until you have achieved the desired colour.

3 Test the colour at intervals by painting out the glaze on to paper. You should only need small amounts of stainer to create the required colour.

Colour Terms

Pure colour

Tint = pure colour + white

Shade = pure colour + black

preparation of glazes. Make notes of the tinter(s) used in the preparation of the colours, recording approximate quantities, and brush out the glaze or wash on to small sample sheets of paper or adhesive plastic. These will be useful for future reference.

Before progressing to the techniques of applying coloured paints and glazes to various surfaces, it is important to understand how colours can be formulated and combined, and the different effects that those colour combinations can produce.

Putting theory into practice is the most effective way of learning. Therefore, it is strongly recommended that those who last tackled colour in the classroom should avail themselves of a basic set of artists' paints, in oil- and water-based colours. Not only do they contain the relevant paints, solvents, brushes and instructions necessary for a quick sortie into colour theory, they also find their exact domestic equivalents in the popular household paints. Emulsions (latex paints) equate with water colours or gouache; undercoat, eggshells and glosses with artists' oils.

CHARACTERISTICS OF COLOUR

Colour has three dimensions: hue, chromatic intensity and tonal value. Hue is the quality by which we differentiate one colour from another. For example, is a colour red or yellow, or green or blue? Chromatic intensity is the strength of a colour, and relates to its brilliance or saturation – or how concentrated it is. Tonal value is a measure of a colour's luminosity or its lightness value. Is it a bright or dark colour? Thus yellow, which is a bright colour, is described as having a higher tonal value than red or blue which are darker colours.

The primary colours, or hues, are red, blue and yellow. In theory they are pure and cannot be made from mixing other colours. The secondary colours, such as orange, purple and green, are made by mixing two primaries together. The tertiary colours, such as red-purple, blue-purple, blue-green, yellow-green, yellow-orange and red-orange, are a mixture of primary and secondary colours.

In theory it is possible to create any colour from combining the three primaries, but in practice the more colours combined together, the more the produced colour will lose its luminosity or vitality. For this reason, artists' suppliers offer a comprehensive range of pure colours, which are far more vibrant.

To familiarise yourself with the jargon of colour mixing try out the following definitions, using your set of colours:

☐ A tint is produced when white is added to a colour.

☐ A shade is produced when black is added to a colour.

☐ A tone is a lighter or darker version of the same colour.

☐ Warm colours are those that tend towards red.

☐ Cold colours are those that tend towards blue. (As a qualification, reds containing small amounts of blue, such as cerise, can be cold. In the same way blues containing small amounts of red, such as duck-egg blue, can be warm.)

☐ Complementary colours are those which are opposite one another on the colour wheel. Mixed in equal proportions they will neutralise one another and produce a grey. Mixed in disproportionate amounts they will take the heat or warmth out of the dominant colour. Again, while this may work in theory, in practice it results in the colour losing much of its intensity. An alternative method of toning-down a colour is to add one of the 'earth' colours that contains its complementary, such as raw umber, raw sienna or burnt umber.

☐ Discordant colours are different hues that are brought tonally close together by tinting or shading; that is, by the addition of black or white. The resulting colours, when juxtaposed, are known as discordant. An example would be when yellow shaded with black is positioned next to a deep blue tinted with white.

☐ Off-hues are created when colours that are similar, but not actually adjacent on the colour wheel (see below right), are placed side by side.

Transparency and colour

The various rules and examples that have been discussed so far relate to colour as seen in an opaque state. Opacity or covering power is the ability of a paint to obscure the ground colour over which it is applied, and is generally a guide to the density of pigment and the quality and cost of the paint. While this feature is of use in the preparation of ground coats, it is the ability of paint to retain the vitality and intensity of its colour in the transparent state, as a glaze or wash, that is of far greater importance to the decorative painter.

Whilst the preparation of glazes is straightforward, the variables involved when combining coloured glazes over contrasting, opaque grounds becomes so infinitely subtle that the formulation of precise rules is not only impractical but impossible. However, there are some basic guidelines you can follow. Glazes that are deeper in value than the ground will increase the warmth of a surface, provided the ground remains luminous or translucent. Whereas a light neutral glaze over a dark surface produces a warm intensity. And a light glaze thinly applied over a dark tone produces a cold surface.

When a glaze is applied over an opaque ground, the world of broken colour techniques (see pages 62-75) is entered.

Colour and marble

The colour qualities of marble are discussed on pages 96-8. In all the marbles that I have ever inspected, I have never come across an unfortunate colour combination – Mother Nature simply doesn't make mistakes. Real marbles combine harmonious, complementary colours. However, many modern marble fantasies fly in the face of nature, using jarring, discordant colours and off-hues to create their impact.

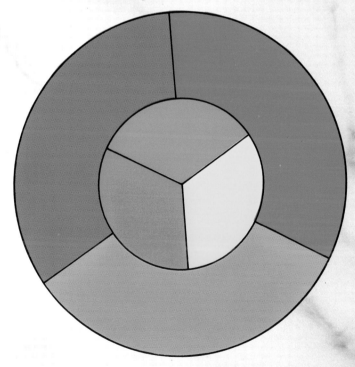

This colour wheel illustrates the relationship between the colours. Neighbouring hues are harmonious and those opposite are contrasting.

4

THE BROKEN COLOUR TECHNIQUES

This chapter details various 'broken colour' techniques, taken from the fields of decorative painting and fine art, and shows how they are used in the marbling process. Whilst some of them are able to imply a marble surface in their own right, most of them must be combined to produce an authentic or credible marble illusion.

A familiarity with the techniques will provide a blueprint for systematically tackling specific marbles and fantasy effects (which are covered in Chapter Seven: Starting to Marble).

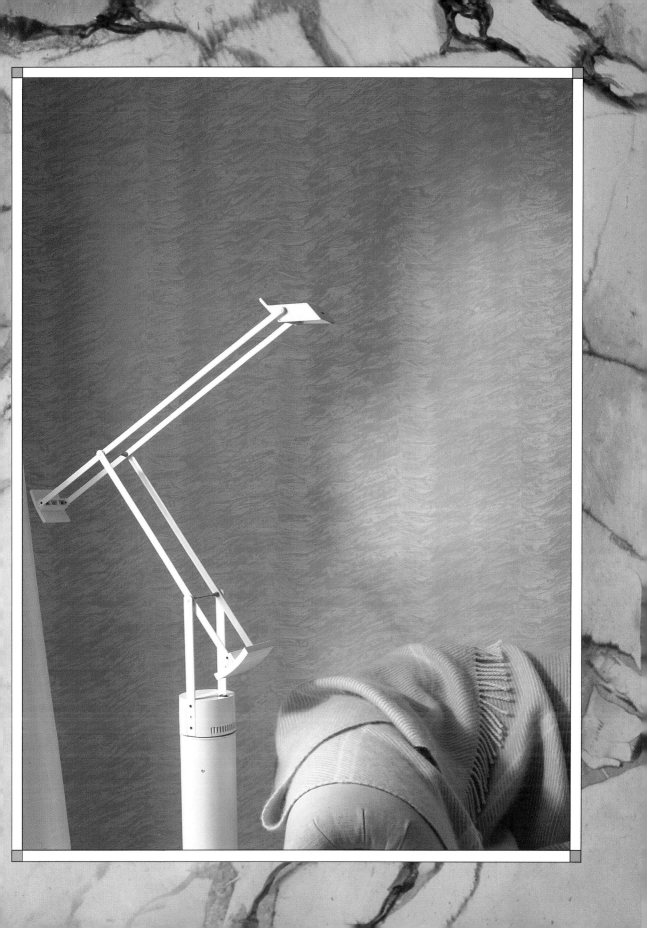

WHAT DOES BROKEN COLOUR MEAN?

Broken colour is simply a film of paint or glaze which is neither continuous nor evenly distributed over a surface. The various techniques offer formal ways of patterning both this film and the ground coat underneath it.

'Distressing the surface' is the phrase used to describe the various ways in which broken colour is created, and the 'distressing tool' is the implement used to apply or displace the paint or glaze. Its form contributes to the appearance of the effect or illusion.

There are two distinct methods for creating broken colour: the additive and the subtractive methods.

The additive method

To a previously prepared, opaque coloured ground, a contrasting glaze is applied using the selected distressing tool, such as a sponge or cloth.

The subtractive method

This involves applying the prepared glaze to the entire surface of the opaque ground, usually with a brush. Whilst the glaze remains wet, or 'alive', it is distressed with the selected tool, such

Sponging on
Use a marine sponge soaked in solvent to dab on glaze.

Ragging
Dip a lint-free rag, rolled into a loose ball, in glaze, then apply to the surface with a dabbing and rolling action.

as a comb or sponge, and glaze is removed from or displaced on the surface to produce the required pattern.

SPONGING

A sponge may be used to add or subtract a glaze. In both cases a tight, speckled appearance will result. A less formal and less insistent print will be produced by using a natural, marine sponge instead of its artificial, nylon counterpart.

The size of the sponge will be determined by the area that you wish to tackle, although anything bigger than the size of your fist becomes unmanageable. It is advisable to have a small selection.

The sponge should be soaked in the appropriate solvent (white/mineral spirit for oil-based glaze and water for emulsions) before use, and then thoroughly wrung out.

When using the sponge to apply glaze, don't overcharge it. Remove excess glaze on the side of the container. When using the sponge to remove glaze, clean it regularly in solvent and dry it off on paper or cloth. With both methods, a build-up of glaze in the sponge will cause smudging.

Although a dabbing action is usually employed when sponging, it is generally accompanied by a wrist-rolling action. Always test the effect on rough paper before applying it to the surface in question.

Sponged finishes applied over large areas can produce marble-like finishes, especially if contrasting tonal overlays of the same colour are superimposed.

The speckled print produced by a marine sponge is used in the preparation of granite and porphyry effects.

RAGGING

A rag, of virtually any lint-free material, may be used to add or subtract a glaze. A highly individual print will be formed; its appearance depending on the nature of the material, the way it is bunched in the hand, and the manner in which it is moved over the surface.

Ragging can produce effects that range from a tightly regimented and insistent pattern (see below right), to a loosely applied glaze that leaves no recognisable pattern.

Used additively, first roll the cloth into a loose ball that can be comfortably held in the hand. Pick up glaze on the cloth, removing excess on the side of the container, and, with a dabbing and rocking action, apply the paint to the surface. Varying the pressure and direction, and reforming the cloth, will prevent the print becoming overstated.

Used subtractively, the effect becomes slightly softer, especially if you moisten the cloth with the relevant solvent first. Dab the surface of the wet glaze with a light touch, turning your hand and wrist to avoid forming a repetitive pattern. When the cloth becomes charged with glaze, dispose of it. Employing polythene or greaseproof paper in a similar manner will displace the applied glaze and pro-duce a range of effects remarkably similar to shot silk or crushed velvet.

A variation on the dabbing and turning method is to form the rag into a sausage shape and distress the surface using a rolling action – this is known as rag rolling. Used additively or subtractively, the effect is more formalised, due to the impression of movement and direction apparent in the finish. This method is used to advantage where speed is essential; large areas of fast-drying glazes can be quickly distressed.

When marbling, this technique is a popular method of applying and distressing glazes to create cloudy, marble-like backdrops over large areas, and as such is a fantasy marbling finish in its own right.

Before employing a ragging technique, think carefully about the effect you wish to achieve. The same finish on woodwork and walls may camouflage the wood, putting the shape of the room into softer focus. Make sure that this suits your scheme.

COMBING

A subtractive technique, combing produces a formal finish. The different combs (available from specialist dec-

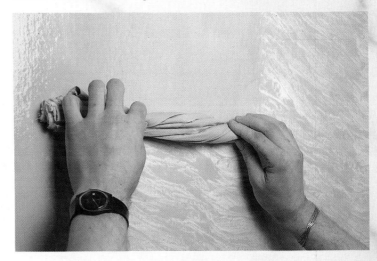

Rag-rolling
Roll a lint-free rag into a sausage shape, dip in glaze, and apply to the surface with a pushing and rolling action.

Combing
Run a decorators' comb through the wet glaze to reveal the ground colour.

Dragging
Pull a dragging brush through wet glaze in a downward motion.

orators' stores, or home-made from cardboard or any semi-rigid material) allow a great variety of prints and patterns to be produced.

The method is simple: merely run the comb through the wet surface so that the glaze is displaced and the ground colour revealed.

Subtle colour contrasts and glaze transparencies are usually subjugated to the insistence of the pattern. Consequently, the technique is best used on furniture, or large areas such as walls or floors, where opaque glazes and bold patterns can create striking and effective abstract designs.

When marbling, the technique may be used to represent the regimented parallel strata effects exhibited in many decorative stones, such as malachite (see page 116), rhodocrosite (see page 122) and yellow onyx (see page 119).

DRAGGING

A subtractive technique, dragging produces highly formalised finishes of great subtlety. The use of a specialist 'dragging' brush gives a uniformly distressed surface, but avoids the regimented, pinstripe effects produced by standard paint brushes.

The method is simple, but requires a

certain mechanical repetitiveness. The brush is dragged through the wet glaze in a systematic and continuous series of parallel downward motions.

This technique is used extensively in woodgraining, and for large wall areas where an elegant and sophisticated finish is required. It has limited application to marbling, but is sometimes used as a stylized backdrop in the preparation of fantasy porphyrys.

STIPPLING

A subtractive technique, stippling involves lifting small quantities of wet glaze from the surface on to the bristles of a stippling brush. Stippling large areas requires the use of a specialist, flat-faced brush. Small areas may be stippled with any brush that has a reasonably flat head of stiff bristles (for example, a 'hog's hair softener' or a 'jam duster').

Over large wall areas uniformly distressed finishes can be produced by rhythmically striking the flat head of the brush against the wet glaze. The brush should be cleaned in solvent at regular intervals to prevent smudging.

A more adventurous approach involves using the technique to create

Stippling
Strike the head of a stippling brush against the wet glaze, thereby lifting small quantities of paint from the surface.

Spattering
Load a stiff-bristled brush with glaze, and strike the shaft against a hard edge to fleck droplets onto the surface.

shading effects, or subtle gradations of colour. Bands of wet glaze are juxtaposed. These may be different colours, or different tones of the same colour. The stippling brush is then used to transfer flecks of glaze from one area to another, thus feathering-out or blurring the adjoining edges.

Stippling can also be used to disguise brush strokes, level out glazes, and blend and tone colours that have been combined on the surface. The latter being particularly useful when working with water-based glazes, which are difficult to blend using a conventional softening brush.

As you will discover, stippling has applications at every stage of the marbling process.

SPATTERING
An additive technique, spattering involves flicking small spots of wet glaze on to a dry, opaque, contrasting ground coat.

There are no formal rules governing the paint, tools or equipment required. Consequently, the technique allows a great variety of individual expression.

Usually, a glaze is loaded on to a stiff bristled brush, such as a stencil or tooth-brush. By running a thumb over the bristles, or striking the shaft of the brush on a hard edge, flecks of paint are spattered on to the surface.

The technique can be controlled quite accurately, and contrasting, superimposed glazes can be built up quickly to produce a fine speckled, multi-coloured finish.

More abstract effects can be produced by flicking opaque gobs of paint on to large areas of wall or floor. The effect does tend to be rather overstated and difficult to control, but is popular in ultra-modern interiors.

When marbling, the technique is used to good effect in the preparation of tight, repetitive, multi-coloured finishes, such as porphyries and granites. Also, it is a good way of introducing small spots of sparsely displayed colour, such as metallic particles, that are sometimes found at the intersections of major veins.

COLOUR WASHING
This technique involves washing thinned glazes over a surface. It is a useful method of slightly modifying underlying colours, and the quick drying time allows further applications to be

Colour washing (above)
Using a large brush, paint a
thinned glaze over the surface.

Cissing by brush (below)
Apply a glaze to the surface,
and while it is still wet load a
stiff brush with solvent. Strike
the brush against a hard edge to
spatter drops of solvent at
random over the glaze.

made in swift succession. The effect is cumulative; the colour deepening with each application.

When marbling, it is used extensively to tone down finishes at the end of the technique. Washes, formed from the predominant colours that have been used, are painted over the surface with a large brush. The resultant toning-down of strident contrasts has a cohesive effect.

CISSING

The technique involves the application of an appropriate solvent to the surface of a wet glaze; that is, white (mineral) spirit or turpentine to oil-based glaze, and water to emulsion (latex) glaze. However, methylated spirits (denatured alcohol) can take the place of water as a cissing agent if the 'solvent resist' method is used.

The process is both quick and simple, and produces a range of attractive features that are often found in the surface of polished marble. Also, it provides a practical way of merging coloured glazes that are applied simultaneously to a surface – after cissing, a gentle stippling with a dry, flat-faced brush is used to even out the colours. Wherever features are too heavily stated or detailed, cissing will soften the effect and produce a cloudy, veiled transparency.

The effects are achieved by the glaze dispersing as the solvent is applied, and in so doing revealing the coloured ground beneath. On the edges of the dispersed glaze 'fringing' occurs; that is, beautiful tonal gradations appear in the coloured glaze. Where the glaze incorporates more than one colour, the solvent creates subtle, banded hues from the various components.

It is the manner in which the solvent is introduced on to the surface that determines the patterns or designs that are produced.

Whichever method you employ (see below), when large amounts of solvent have been introduced on to the surface and it becomes necessary to terminate cissing, any excess should be soaked-up with the tip of some absorbent paper or a cotton bud (Q-tip). Dabbing the surface will lift and smudge the glaze; so be very careful.

By brush

The most common method of cissing is to release small droplets of solvent on

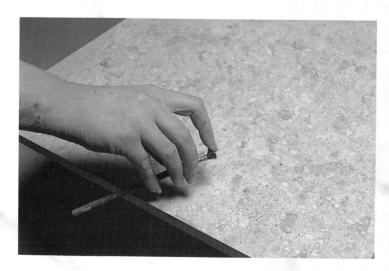

Cissing by brush (above)
Flick the head of the brush with a finger to spatter drops of the solvent over the glaze.

Softening and blending (below)
Wet glaze can be merged and blended by gently pulling a hog's hair softener across the surface.

to the surface by spattering (see page 67). After a little practice the spread of the droplets can be controlled quite effectively. Where each droplet meets the wet surface, the glaze disperses into 'rings' or 'pools', revealing the ground colour in tight, regular circles.

An alternative, and far more precise method of cissing is to take up solvent on the bristles of a stiff brush and dab the glaze with a stippling action (see page 66). The effect can be varied by altering the length of time the brush remains in contact with the glaze. Pulling a soft brush loaded with solvent

through the glaze will produce a very dramatic effect. The glaze will open up to produce a veining effect. Adjusting the pressure on the head of the brush will determine the amount of solvent released, and the subsequent width of the vein.

As vapour

This method consists of blowing solvent on to the surface of the wet glaze, using a paint atomiser (a device available from art shops). The droplets are minute, and the intricate effect resembles the crystallized surface of many of the more sugary textured marbles.

The technique is best used on small items of furniture. However, where it is required on a larger scale, a plant spray with an adjustable nozzle will prove a useful tool; but experiment first, as the effects are difficult to control.

By paper

Dip crisp or stiff paper, such as greaseproof or brown wrapping paper, in a small tray of solvent. Then screw up the paper into a tight ball, unravel it and lay it on the surface of the wet glaze. Depress it slightly for a few seconds, with a flat board, and the solvent will gather where the pleats of the paper touch the glaze. The glaze will open up to produce intricate, angular, veining patterns.

Alternatively, the paper may be formed into a ball or sausage, and rolled over the surface to provide a more controlled and localised effect.

A tennis ball carries solvent well, and will produce similar effects. If the surface you are working on can be tilted, the rolling ball will produce gentle arcs, or interesting parallel repeats.

By sponge

A small piece of marine sponge, dipped

The effect of softening
In real marble, veins deep in
the stone appear blurred and
indeterminate. Softening will
reproduce this effect.

will be necessary to purchase a specialist brush, known as a hog's hair
softener. This is an expensive but versatile tool. After use it must be cleaned
with white (mineral) spirit, washed in
warm, soapy water and hung up to dry.
A more pricey alternative is the badger
softener. Although its fine bristles are
more suited for use with water-based
paints, they produce delicate prints in
oils and are a joy to use.

The oil-based method

To a prepared surface, ideally an oil-
based eggshell ground, apply a thin
coat of scumble glaze (flatting oil),
with a cloth. This may be used neat, or
slightly thinned with white (mineral)
spirit, in a ratio of five parts scumble to
one part spirit. This may be thought of
as a lubricating layer on which to float
the coloured glazes.

Next prepare two or three contrasting glazes, and dab them on in adjoining random patches, using a brush or
cloth. The hog's hair softener is then
pulled gently across the glazes, to
induce the coloured pigments to
merge. After a while the bristles will
become charged with glaze, so they
should be cleaned regularly to stop the
brush skidding.

The brush may also be used to stipple
the merged glazes (see page 66),
thereby levelling them and producing a
slightly softer effect. You will find that
the glazes remain mobile and workable
for some time. However, when the surface becomes sticky, as it starts to harden, don't attempt further softening.

When this process is applied to an
entire surface, it is described as 'scumbling the ground'. This is a standard
method for creating the cloudy, imprecise backgrounds evident in the major-
ity of marbles. When a scumbled
ground has hardened off, detailed

in solvent and dabbed on to the wet
glaze, provides a useful and controllable method of cissing.

SOFTENING AND BLENDING

Elements that lie close to the surface of
polished marble, such as veins or fossils, are clearly identifiable. However,
as they recede into the body of the
stone their images blur and fade, until
eventually they are lost to view in a
swirling sea of indeterminate colour
and form. The impression of mystery
and depth that this effect lends to the
polished surface is captured by the
technique of softening and blending.

Although the process is applicable to
both the oil- and water-based systems,
the success of the technique relies, to a
great extent, on the ability to induce
coloured pigments to merge in a controlled fashion. This requires a relatively slow-drying surface, and a fairly
substantial glaze medium. In both
these respects the water-based system is
inferior to the oil-based one, and
comes a second best in the preparation
of sophisticated simulations. However,
it does have certain merits.

In order to operate the technique it

features may then be applied using more opaque colour.

For more localised work, where you need to exercise greater control over the effects, mix the coloured glazes with a substantial amount of thinned scumble glaze, before applying them to the prepared surface.

To produce a thinned scumble glaze mix the scumble with white (mineral) spirit, in a ratio of one to one. Then mix this with the coloured glazes in a ratio of, approximately, one part thinned scumble to three parts coloured glaze.

Once again, softening and blending will cause the colours to merge.

The water-based method

The technique of softening and blending in water-based colour is far more difficult than in oils. However, the use of a badger softener, rather than a hog's hair brush, will help.

Emulsion (latex) grounds are uneven and porous, and will dry out thinned glazes before the technique can be applied. Therefore, undercoat or eggshell oil-based grounds should be applied. These must be keyed with 1000 grade wet and dry paper soaked in warm, soapy water.

Working in an atmosphere that is neither too dry nor too warm, apply the prepared water-based glazes in small, manageable-sized patches to the surface, and begin softening and blending immediately. In order to achieve a smooth gradation of pigments from one glaze to the next, it is necessary to combine the technique with a stippling action (see page 66). A few drops of liquid detergent added to the thinned glaze will prevent it from 'gathering', and will provide slightly more mobility on the surface.

Acrylic, water-based colour may

Applying scumble
Dip a cloth in thinned scumble glaze and wipe over the ground.

prove a more suitable alternative as there are two proprietary products that may be added to ease the process of softening and blending. A retarder may be added to slow the drying time (see page 57); for earth colours, the recommended mix is one part retarder to six parts paint, and for other colours, it is one part retarder to three parts paint. Alternatively, acrylic matt medium may be added to further thin acrylic glazes, increase translucency without sacrificing the matt quality of the paint, give the glaze more 'body', and facilitate pigment mobility over the ground coat.

ISOLATING

This technique may be used at any stage during the marbling process. The object is to seal the delicate surfaces against the effects of further, superimposed glazes or distressing techniques by applying a protective cover of transparent varnish. The varnish may be thought of as a thin layer of glass through which the painted ground can be clearly seen.

Its most common application is in the sealing of scumbled grounds that are made from water-based colour (see

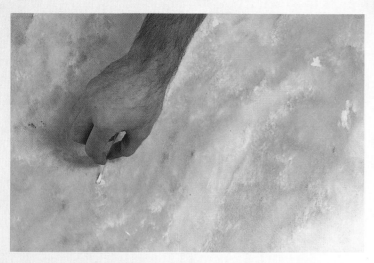

*Wiping out
Use a cotton bud (Q-tip)
moistened with solvent to
displace wet glaze and reveal
the ground colour.*

page 58). Without it, the application of further water-based glazes would put previously applied pigments back into solution, and thereby ruin the effect.

Isolating is also used to protect both oil and water-based finishes that will be subjected to extensive cissing (see page 68) and/or wiping out (see page 72) procedures, where the surface would suffer actual physical damage.

The method involves the application of one or more coats of transparent varnish to the surface, which must be completely hard and dry. Time must be allowed between coats of varnish for each layer to dry out completely.

Two types of varnish may be used: 'white polish', or matt or mid-sheen polyurethane varnish.

White polish has the advantage of drying quickly, allowing several coats to be applied in a matter of minutes. When dry, this polish may be gently sanded, with fine sandpaper, to level out any imperfections in the surface and underlying paint. The major disadvantage is that it is a relatively unstable product, being readily dissolved by both alcohol and water. Consequently, if you intend to apply any water-based glazes over it, you must

first apply a thin layer of matt polyurethane varnish for protection.

On the other hand, polyurethane varnish provides a durable, transparent surface. However, it is relatively slow drying, so it should be thinned with white (mineral) spirit to speed up the drying rate, and any superimposed glazes should only be applied after it has completely dried out. Subsequently applied water-based glazes will require the addition of small quantities of detergent, to prevent them coalescing or gathering on the surface.

WIPING OUT

This technique allows you to remove or displace sections of an applied glaze whilst it is still wet, so that the ground beneath may be seen. Where the glaze is wiped back to reveal a white or pale ground, subsequently applied glazes achieve a far greater luminosity.

Care must be taken when wiping out water-based paint that has been applied to a water-based ground. This is because the underlying pigment in the ground could be put back into solution when aggravated by the wiping out procedure.

The usual method is to remove sections of glaze from the surface by wiping out with a dry, clean cloth, or one that has been moistened with the appropriate solvent.

Alternatively, the glaze may be displaced on the surface using a cloth wrapped around the forefinger, or by moving some object, such as a cork or pencil eraser, over the surface. The object should have no sharp edges that may gouge the underlying finish.

Also, the glaze may be lifted or displaced using various items such as pieces of string, sectioned vegetables and half-inflated balloons. In fact, any item you regard as suitable can be used, provided it is clean and dry. The object is to leave a reverse print in the glaze which will represent the various repeated patterns or elements, such as fossils or large crystals, featured in marble surfaces.

VEINING
Perhaps the most decorative, dramatic and expressive feature evident in the surface of polished stone is veining. An understanding of the manner in which veins are formed will prove invaluable to their simulation (see page 15).

To assist in the understanding of this phenomenon, take the analogy of a block of ice that has been struck with a hammer: stress fractures radiate out in all directions from the point of impact. If a coloured dye was introduced at this point the fluid would trace out the path of the faults, in much the same way as veins are formed in marble. You will notice that the the veins are strongly stated at the point of impact, but as they extend through the ice they dissipate and fade to thin lines.

In marble itself, some veins emerge from the depths to become bold and obvious; whilst others retreat from the surface and dissolve into a cloudy, imprecise background. You will find that veins rarely form arcs or double-back on themselves; their lines tend to be angular and jagged, and their width is not constant.

Where a veining pattern lies on, or just below the surface of a composition, there is little to choose between the oil- and water-based systems. However, where the vein must advance towards, or retreat from, the surface, the techniques of softening and blending (see pages 69-71) and stippling (see page 66) must be used to soften the image. These techniques are far more effective and controllable when using the oil-

based system.

Nevertheless, the quick-drying, water-based system is ideal for achieving fast results in those areas that are not subject to close inspection, such as floors or corridors. The image may be softened by stippling the vein (see page 66) immediately after it has been painted in.

You will discover that veins and veining patterns are capable of projecting great strength of line. Consequently, in order not to overstate their presence they must, for the most part, be represented in softly muted colours. However, some veins that lie on the surface should be clearly stated in sharp, opaque colour; a process generally regarded as detailing, and added as a finishing touch to a painted simulation.

There are many methods of simulating veins, and some of the most popular are described on the following pages. However, the list is far from complete; so there is plenty of scope for personal innovation.

By brush
Brushes are the most obvious and, in many ways, the most versatile choice.

Veining by brush
Holding a fine artists' brush well up the handle, adjust the pressure on the bristles to vary the width of the vein.

Artists' shops provide an enormous range of fine brushes suitable for the task. Build up a selection of different sizes, best suited to your needs; but be warned, some can be very pricey.

Although no two people use a brush in exactly the same manner, in order to capture the imprecise, meandering qualities of a vein, it is advisable to hold the brush well up the shaft with a fairly light grip, between the thumb and forefinger.

Try to tease the paint on to the surface, rather than making a bold stroke. Hold the brush at an angle to the work, and adjust the pressure on the bristles to vary the width of the vein.

When using a round brush, rolling the shaft will cause slight variations in the transparency of the applied glaze. When using a flat-faced brush, the object is to 'fidget' the paint on to the surface using a dithering, side-to-side movement.

Flat brushes may be charged with two contrasting glazes, on adjacent sides of the brush head. Rolling the brush and varying the pressure on the bristles can create veins of great subtlety, with the colours either remaining separate, or merging to form attractive

Veining by feather
Moisten the feather in solvent, pick up the glaze on the fronds, then sweep the glaze across the surface of the ground.

Veining by crayon
Use the tip of the crayon for fine detail; turn it on its side to create an undulating vein.

graduated hues.

If you charge a brush with solvent and pull it through a wet glaze, the paint will ciss (see page 68) and a veining channel will open up. This can then be tinted with a contrasting coloured glaze. Where cissing has revealed the ground coat, a coloured glaze painted into the channel will exhibit greater luminosity.

By feather

Goose feathers provide a useful alternative to the brush. They may be found in plenty near stretches of inland water.

To prepare the feather place it in water, and split the fronds or blade with your thumb nail into the required formation. The smaller the sections, the sketchier the veins will be.

Used as a sweeping blade, with the fronds split into many fine sections, the feather will produce intricate networks of fine, interconnecting veins. Before picking up the glaze on the fronds, the feather should be moistened with the appropriate solvent (see page 68).

Usually, the tip of the feather is left intact, as laid flat on the surface it provides an excellent tool for quickly applying very thin layers of paint over

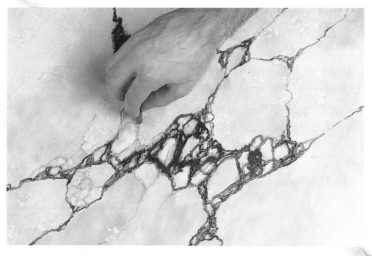

relatively large areas. On its edge, it may be used like an italic nib to produce delicate, undulating veins.

A few minutes experimentation will reveal the great potential and versatility of this simple tool.

By coloured crayons and soft pastels

These are applicable to both the oil- and water-based systems, and provide a quick and easy method of applying fine, opaque detail to the finished work. Equally, where the marbling is to be pale and translucent, they may be used directly on the prepared ground to create features that will be clearly visible through the superimposed glazes.

The crayon may be used on its tip to produce fine detail, or on its side in order to create a gently undulating, softly stated vein.

When working with water-based colours, crayons, soft pastels and charcoal can be used at any stage of the process, provided the surface is dry. Recommended fixatives, or white polish (see page 71), should be used to isolate the finish locally, preventing any solvent reaction in the superimposed glazes.

Conté crayons are pure pigments bound in oil, and these may be used with the oil-based system whether the surface of the work is wet or dry. To a limited degree their appearance may be softened and blended (see page 70) with a brush.

By cottons and twines

Cottons or twines may be used individually, or combined to form tassels in order to distress the surface. The object is to produce thin, filament-like veins, or complex, intermeshing patterns. Used dry, or dipped in the appropriate solvent (see page 68), they may be used to displace, remove or ciss (see page 67) a glaze on the surface.

When charged with glaze, they may be laid on the surface and gently pressed with a clean cloth to induce the release of paint; or, as a tassel, used to flog the work to produce a wispy, delicate pattern.

By knotted string or net

Used additively or subtractively, string bags, fishing net or net curtaining can be very effective tools for reproducing the regimented, veining patterns of some marbles.

Rip the net, to prevent the pattern from becoming too strident, and dab the wet glaze to remove and displace it. Alternatively, moisten the net with solvent or glaze, and lay it precisely on the surface in the shape of the required pattern; then carefully remove it. The net can also be positioned on the surface as a stencil, and sprayed with aerosol paint (see page 69). This is a particularly effective method of producing abstract fantasy marbles.

By frayed rope

Select some pieces of hemp rope, of varying thicknesses. Fray the ends, and unravel the rope so that its thickness varies along its length. Holding the rope as flat as possible against a firm surface, liberally apply some quick-drying varnish, such as white polish (see page 71). As the varnish hardens you will be able to organise the strands more effectively. Apply a further two coats, to make the frayed rope fairly rigid. Prepare as many ropes as you may require in this fashion.

Lay the prepared ropes on the surface you are marbling, to the required pattern, and mist aerosol paint over them. This technique works like a stencil, to produce all manner of veining systems.

5

PREPARING SURFACES

This chapter deals with the preparation of various surfaces which you are likely to encounter when marbling. These may vary from a perfectly flat and smooth glass vase, to an uneven, bumpy and flaking plaster wall.

Whilst the correct preparation will ensure that all surfaces can take paint, it must be accepted that, however good the technique, some will never be able to provide a good enough ground for an authentic marble finish.

ASSESSING THE SURFACE

Polished marble is very flat. So, whilst small irregularities, gouges and dents in a surface may prove fiddly and awkward to repair, it is the shallow, undulating ripples that are the most distracting in a finish, especially over large flat surfaces, such as walls.

You can assess the extent of these ripples by placing your eye close to the surface, and looking towards a light source; they will be immediately evident. Alternatively, a long 'straight edge' may be used. Imperfections on the vertical plane are far more critical than those on the horizontal, unless the surface is artificially lit directly from above, with, for example, a wall-mounted fitting.

There are no hard and fast rules with regard to the suitability of the surface. It is really a matter of common sense. If your intention is the authentic replication of a specific marble then few, if any, surface imperfections can be tolerated. If, on the other hand, perfection is not your aim, an impressive result can still be obtained on an imperfect surface, provided certain guidelines are followed.

Disguising poor surfaces

Certain surface imperfections can be incorporated as features into the pattern of the painted illusion. Gouges, scratches and dents can form the focal points for a complex series of veined intersections. In the natural material it is at such intersections that the surface is often seen to be physically degrading and crumbling.

Cracks in plaster are another obvious ground for a veining system. They may also be used to suggest a fault line, where strata have become disjointed and then rewelded.

Wallpaper joints that stand out can be disguised as panel joins, or incorporated as a surrounding border. Surfaces that are heavily textured or embossed with regular patterns can be swiftly disguised by uniformly distressing the surface. Here, the object is to produce a coloured background, using a paint technique such as rag rolling or stippling (see pages 64-75), which distracts the eye from any surface relief, and provides a backdrop on which to construct marble details. Fast-drying matt emulsions (latex paints) are ideal for use in such situations.

Any reflective surface will tend to emphasise underlying imperfections. Gloss varnish, in particular, is most revealing. So, if a protective varnish is to be used, rely on the matt or midsheen varieties. Where it is absolutely essential to take advantage of the protective qualities of gloss, its surface may be 'knocked back' by lightly wet and drying with 1200 grade grit carborundum paper.

PREPARATION OF WALLS

Walls are the most visually important surface in a room. Much of their surface is at eye level and it is therefore subject to close scrutiny. Where quality simulations are proposed the preparation should be scrupulous.

Assess how true the wall is by applying a 2 metre (6½ foot) straight edge to the surface. If large, undulating ripples are evident replastering will be necessary. Remember to check in vertical and horizontal directions.

Paint on plaster

Provided the painted surface is sound, it will only require washing with warm soapy water and disinfectant, followed by a rinse with clean water. Kitchens may require additional scrubbing to remove grease, and if there is any mould or discoloration evident a proprietary fungicide must be added to the wash. Gloss paint must be keyed with an abrasive, such as wet and dry paper, before applying an undercoat.

If the painted surface contains a pattern, and the marbling technique requires a white ground, it is advisable to paint out the old finish with a darker shade, before applying the undercoat. Otherwise the pattern may show through, or even bleed into, the white; reds are especially prone to this. To avoid the problem completely, seal with a knotting compound before applying the white.

Localised flaking paint can be treated by rubbing down and feathering out the edges, using medium-grade sandpaper. If this produces more flaking, lightly abrade the surrounding area, seal with a proprietary surface sealer or stabilizer, and make a small repair with 'fine-grade' surface filler (spackle). Apply it as a thin film using a flat, plastic spreader. When the filler (spackle) has hardened, lightly abrade it with a fine-grade sandpaper and then re-seal.

If flaking is widespread, and the layers of paint are quite thick, the most practical solution is to seal the entire surface and cover the wall with heavy-duty lining paper.

Wallpaper

If the paper is in good condition, and shows no signs of lifting or discoloration, it should be wiped over with warm, soapy water and disinfectant, and then sealed with emulsion (latex) or undercoat.

Lifting wallpaper can be treated locally by injecting wallpaper paste through a hole pierced in the bubble using a plastic syringe. Alternatively,

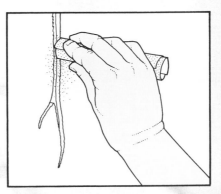

1) Clean up the hole or crack and chamfer the edges using medium-grade sandpaper.

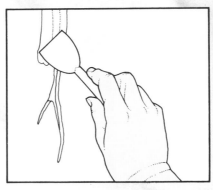

2) Apply a proprietary filler (spackle) to the crack using a flat plastic spreader. The filler should sit slightly proud of the surrounding surface.

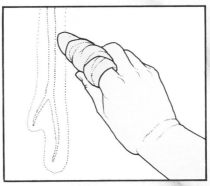

3) Before the filler has hardened, use a damp cloth wrapped round your finger to wipe off any excess on the surrounding surface.

4) When the filler has hardened, lightly abrade it with fine-grade sandpaper until the surface is level.

the lifting section can be cut out with a blade and another piece let-in. Lifting seams should be reseated, after applying paste with a small brush.

Paper that is heavily embossed or in poor condition should be stripped. For large areas, stripping machines are available for hire. Try not to damage the underlying plaster surface.

Vinyl papers are not a suitable surface on which to apply emulsion undercoats. They should be stripped, or undercoated with oil-based paint.

Bare plaster

New plaster surfaces require sealing with a watered-down emulsion (latex), prior to undercoating. Old but sound plaster surfaces are suitable for oil- or water-based paints, and matt emulsion paint or undercoat provides a suitable ground coat.

Large holes or cracks should be cleaned and their edges chamfered. The surrounding area should be abraded with medium grade sandpaper, and a proprietary filler (spackle), in the form of a thick paste, should be applied with a plastic spreader so that it sits slightly proud of the surface. Before it has hardened, a damp cloth wrapped around the forefinger may be used to wipe off any excess on the surrounding surface. After the repair has hardened, level the surface, using medium grit sandpaper. A straight-edged steel rule laid across the surface will indicate how flat the repair is. A fine grade surface filler (spackle) should be used to add the finishing touches. Seal the repair with matt emulsion (latex) paint or undercoat.

PREPARATION OF FLOORS

The visual strength of a marbled floor lies in the colour combinations and contrasts evident in the geometric panel design, rather than in the perfection of the surface. Consequently, any repairs need not be quite so meticulous as for walls.

Concrete floors

Usually, solid floors only require superficial repair work to make them ideal surfaces on which to marble. Although the effect of undulating ripples will not be that pronounced, it is as well to try and identify any large imperfections. A straight edge or a round ball placed on the surface will seek out any hollows. Self-levelling screeds may be used for major repair work. For small repairs use a proprietary filler (spackle). Apply a continuous coat of linoleum paint to seal any repairs and imperfections. This will provide a smooth surface on which to construct a marbling ground.

Vinyl tiles

Provided the surface of the tiles is not over-textured or highly embossed, it will provide a good surface on which to marble. Tiles should be washed with hot soapy water, thoroughly dried and sealed with a polyurethane sealant.

The main drawback is the dominant pattern created by the tile junctions. Whilst this could be incorporated into your intended design, where it becomes a distraction a thick linoleum paint may be applied in order to camouflage the joints.

Linoleum

This provides a more continuous surface than tiles. However, it has a tendency to crack, especially if it is old or has been placed over an underlying ridge or fault. Correct these faults, and ensure that any butting edges are flush, and are glued down with a contact adhesive. Cushion-backed linoleum can be used, but the slight 'give' in the

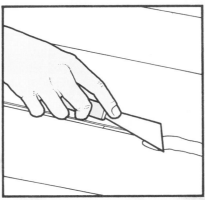

Far left: When marbling floorboards large gaps between the boards should first be bridged using thin wooden slivers. Tack or glue slivers in place and then over-fill them.

Left: There is no need to bridge smaller gaps. Simply fill with a vinyl-based, flexible seam filler.

surface can lead to cracking of the paintwork under the effects of heavy traffic. A proprietary floor paint will be required to seal the surface, before cos-tructing the marble ground.

Ceramic tiles

As with vinyl tiles, the regimented pat-tern repeat can be a restriction on your design. However, it is possible to level off the joins with tile grout or a proprie-tary filler (spackle). The floor should be washed with hot soapy water, and dried thoroughly before filling. Seal the sur-face with floor paint or a proprietary ceramic sealant.

A relatively new innovation has been the introduction of epoxy-based paints which are suitable for repairing and recolouring all manner of ceramic and enamel surfaces. These are avail-able as a two-pack system, in a limited range of colours.

Unpainted floorboards

The strong visual accent of parallel floorboards will present a major prob-lem for anyone wishing to construct an authentic marble design. To overcome this you will probably have to construct a panel system (see pages 86-93).

However, if you do wish to go ahead, floorboards should first be checked to see if they are securely mounted to the joists. Small repairs should be effected using proprietary fillers (spackle), and then sanded flat. Any knots must be sealed with a knotting compound, to prevent resin penetrating the finish. Gaps between boards should be filled with a vinyl-based, flexible seam filler (spackle). Large gaps must first be bridged with thin wooden slivers. These should be tacked or glued into a countersunk position and then over-filled. Ensure that the repair is flush with the adjacent floorboards by level-ling with a straight edge.

Once the repairs are complete, the boards should be lightly sanded, vacuumed to remove traces of dust, and then painted with a wood sealer. Mar-bling may now begin by laying the ground (see page 99).

Painted floorboards

Painted boards that are in good condi-tion should be repaired in the same manner as unpainted boards. Where the repairs reveal the natural wood, you must locally seal the area before laying the ground.

Those in poor condition should be secured to the joists, checked for proud nails, and then bed-sanded using a light industrial tool. These machines may be hired, but be warned, it is a dirty and demanding job.

Where a sticky varnish covers the boards it may be necessary to use a blow torch to burn it off, prior to bed sanding. Local repairs may then be made, after which the seams must be filled and the natural wood sealed, before laying the ground. This is a costly and time consuming task, not to be undertaken lightly. In this situation a panel system might make a sensible alternative (see pages 86-93).

For those who wish to marble a floor, but are somewhat put off by the degree of commitment required, consider the alternative of preparing a small area of detailed marbling, to be positioned centrally as a feature within the room. As far as preparation goes, this should involve far less work.

ARTEFACTS

The range of items suitable for marbling is vast. Consequently, you will have to deal with all manner of materials, especially when fantasy marbling. Any object with a reasonably smooth surface can be prepared to take a painted finish. However, common sense must prevail. Objects with extremely rough or heavily contoured surfaces will prove difficult to prepare to any reasonable standard, and are best left alone.

Paper

Oil- and water-based paints may be applied to most paper surfaces. Those with a heavy, glazed finish should always be undercoated first. Absorbent papers, such as lining paper, that are to be hung before marbling must either be undercoated or, where emulsions (latex paints) are to be used, given a coat of size.

Glass

This surface must be washed with warm soapy water to remove any traces of oil or grease, and thoroughly dried. Glass paints may then be applied directly to the surface. Alternatively, the surface may be undercoated with oil-based paint, prior to marbling with more traditional paints.

Plastics

Wash with warm soapy water, using a light scouring sponge to abrade the surface. Rinse, allow to dry and seal with an oil-based undercoat.

Fibreglass

The quality of the fibreglass surface varies enormously, depending on the manufacturing process. Smooth, hard surfaces require little more than a light sanding and dusting before the application of an undercoat. Surfaces that exhibit small imperfections should be sanded with fine grade sandpaper.

Pin holes, often evident in the surface of fibreglass objects, should be filled with a fine grade filler (spackle), which must be the consistency of cream and applied with an old paint brush using a stippling action. Apply as many coats as are required to level the surface, and after sanding down and blowing off dust apply an undercoat.

An alternative solution is to apply a coat of transparent, fibreglass gel. This is a polyester resin and comes as a two pack system. The gel must be mixed with an exact amount of hardener, before application with a paint brush. There is only a limited amount of time available before the mixture dries. Protective gloves must be worn, and containers and brushes must be thoroughly cleaned in cellulose thinners before the resin hardens. This surface is incredibly tough, and some care should be taken to achieve a flat finish in order to minimize unnecessary sanding after the surface has cured. Please note that these are hazardous chemicals. Health and safety should be paramount; follow the instructions on the container.

Where the glass fibre has a very textured surface, the best solution is to apply a 'high build' primer/sealer (available from auto paint manufacturers). This is particularly useful for applying even coats to a contoured surface. Being cellulose-based, care should be taken to provide adequate ventilation during application and drying. Follow the instructions and safety precautions on the container.

Metal

Painted metal surfaces that are in good condition should be washed with warm soapy water using a light scouring pad, rinsed, allowed to dry and then undercoated.

Painted surfaces that are chipped should be abraded with sandpaper to feather-out hard edges and, if bare metal is exposed, treated locally with a proprietary metal primer. The process is then the same as for sound surfaces.

Surfaces that are heavily pitted with rust should be sand blasted. This is a specialist job, so consult the yellow pages. After treatment the piece must be primed with metal primer and then undercoated.

Wood

Painted surfaces in good condition should be washed with warm soapy water using a light scouring pad, rinsed, wiped dry, rubbed down and then undercoated. Any gloss surface on which you are planning to paint an emulsion (latex) base coat must be abraded with wet and dry paper.

Painted surfaces that are chipped should be dry sanded to feather out hard edges, and locally sealed with a

wood primer. Then continue as for a sound surface.

If the deterioration of the painted surface is widespread, the piece should be completely stripped. If a proprietary chemical stripper is used, or if the piece is stripped professionally in a caustic soda (lye) bath, it must be scrubbed down with diluted acetic acid (vinegar) to neutralise the chemicals. If the paint is removed with a blowlamp be careful not to char the wood, and sand down the bare wood with a medium grade paper. In both cases, apply a proprietary wood sealer before the ground coat of emulsion (latex) or undercoat.

Wood surfaces that are heavily waxed should be abraded with fine grade steel wool soaked in methylated spirits (denatured alcohol). The surface should then be washed in warm soapy water using an abrasive sponge, rinsed, and thoroughly dried. Then, if the grain has been raised, the surface should be rubbed down with a fine grade sandpaper in the direction of the grain and, finally, undercoated.

Hardboard panels

If you decide that the surfaces of your walls or floors are too unsightly, and cannot be retrieved by diligent preparation, you may decide to marble using a panel system (see pages 84-93). When the hardboard panels have been cut to size, it is important that they are properly prepared.

If you intend to marble with water-based paints, the board must be primed with a proprietary sealant. For oil paints use a primer/undercoat.

Before fixing the panels in position, scrub the backs with water and allow them to stand for a day in the room they are intended for. This will allow them to acclimatise, and thereby avoid warping when fixed down.

Feather out hard edges on paint surfaces that are chipped by dry sanding.

Once sanded, seal the chipped area with a wood primer.

6

PANELLING SYSTEMS

Wherever marble is used as a cladding material, such as on walls or floors, the thin veneer is always applied in the form of a simple panel system. Although this method is imposed by the practicalities of cutting, handling and positioning marble, it is an instantly recognisable format that may be used when marbling to add strength and authority to the illusion.

TYPES OF SYSTEM

There are two types of panel system. The first involves working directly on the surface to be decorated, and is known as the 'direct' system. The second is a 'demountable' system, in which individual panels, made of hardboard for example, are cut out, marbled off site and then fixed in position on the surface.

The advantages of the latter system are that unsightly surfaces, which cannot be retrieved by diligent repair and preparation, are hidden from view; marbling can take place on the horizontal, so that thin glazes and neat solvents may be applied in quantity, without fear of runs or sags; and the panels may be used in other situations when the time comes to change the decor.

The disadvantages are ones of additional cost, and the inconvenience of cutting out, supporting and fixing the panels in position.

A panel system is not obligatory. If you feel confident enough in your materials and your ability, there is nothing to stop you tackling entire wall or floor areas in one operation. However, if you subsequently decide to superimpose a panel system by outlining with flat, painted borders, the continuity of your initial work will detract from the panelled effect. The problem is that the natural breaks evident between panels will not, in this case, look particularly convincing.

WALL PANEL SYSTEMS

Before applying the technique to the wall, you must first design a panel system on graph paper. The dimensions of the system will be determined by the size and form of the wall and room. So, the first job is to take accurate dimensions of the surfaces to be decorated.

Transfer these dimensions to graph paper, remembering to include the outline of such features as doors, windows,

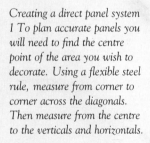

Creating a direct panel system
1 To plan accurate panels you will need to find the centre point of the area you wish to decorate. Using a flexible steel rule, measure from corner to corner across the diagonals. Then measure from the centre to the verticals and horizontals.

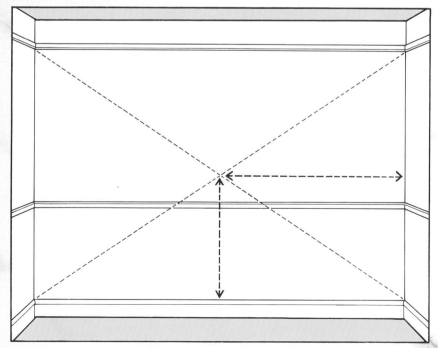

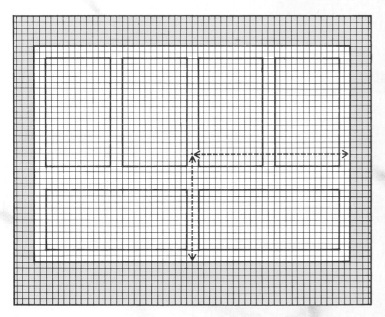

tal rectangular panels will lower it. Panel shapes and positions may be further accentuated by featuring them against contrasting borders in flat paint, a different marbling technique or a stencilled section. You should bear all these factors in mind during the planning stage.

Transferring the design – the direct system

When you are satisfied with the system, scale-up the dimensions of the panels from your graph paper and transfer the outlines, in chalk, on to the wall, which has already been prepared for decoration (see pages 76-83).

Transferring the design – the demountable system

If you intend to use a demountable system, the outlines of your designs must be transferred to the smooth side of hardboard (available from your timber merchant in large sheets). The

2 Transfer the dimensions on to graph paper, then experiment with different panel sizes on tracing overlays until you have a satisfactory group of panel outlines.

dado and picture rails. Overlay with tracing paper, and experiment with possible panel sizes to determine the correct proportions.

Vertical rectangular panels will visually heighten the ceiling; horizon-

3 Use chalk to indicate the panel outlines, scaled-up from the graph paper, on the prepared wall. Now you are ready to add your marbled illusion.

Cutting marble book ends
If a block of marble is cut into
thin laminate panels a similar,
but slightly progressive, pattern
appears in each consecutive
panel.

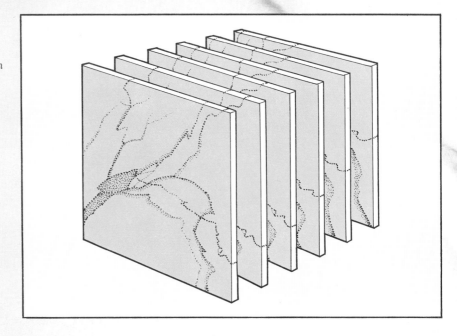

individual panels are cut out using a jig-saw. Make sure you fully support the board to prevent tearing. If you intend to use water-based paints, the board or panels must be sealed with a proprietary wood sealer or undercoat before marbling.

As a safeguard, the panels should be temporarily assembled in front of the wall, to ensure that the system will fit. The boards should always be clearly marked, so that their position on the wall can be easily located.

Composing the panels

Whichever system you intend to use, before tackling the individual panels it is important to establish the position of major areas of colour, and the prominent veining characteristics, of the whole system. Collectively, it is these features that will create the overall visual pattern within the room. Even if your detail work on individual panels is immaculate, if it does not form a harmonious picture, your efforts will have been wasted.

While there is much to commend intuition and flair, it is recommended that you mark out in chalk the prominent features of each panel, before commencing the technique. While mistakes are not terminal, continual restarts can be frustrating and time consuming.

Unfortunately there are no hard and fast rules for ensuring the successful disposition of colour and pattern on panelling. You must rely heavily on your 'artistic eye'.

If you are trying for an authentic simulation, pictures, slides or sketches will prove invaluable, because whilst marble samples are useful for gauging colour, major pattern repeats are sometimes only apparent over large areas. Similarly, if you are preparing a fantasy and you do not wish to make sketches, be sure to carry in your mind's eye a clear idea of the disposition of the major elements that are to be displayed on the panel.

Don't be afraid to produce full-scale trial panels, in emulsion, to test your

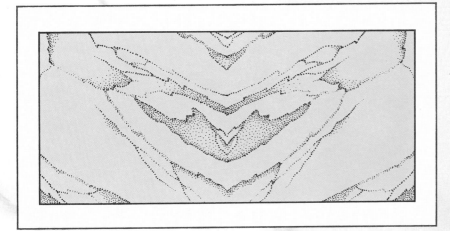

Forming single book ends
If one piece of the consecutive laminate panels (see opposite) is reversed, a mirror image is formed.

Forming double book ends
When two of four consecutive laminate panels (see opposite) are reversed and juxtaposed, a double symmetrical pattern is made.

consecutive panel. Where the laminate is reversed, a mirror image is formed. When panels are juxtaposed in this fashion, in a sequence, they are known as 'book-ends'. A refinement of this phenomenon may involve 'double book-ends', or even a progression of the pattern along an entire wall.

When marbling, using a 'book-end' technique will lend considerable authenticity to the illusion, and has the additional advantage of being a repetitive, and therefore reasonably quick procedure.

Marbling the panels

Assuming that a suitable ground has been prepared (see page 83), use blue chalk to mark out the major design elements of each panel. Prepare sufficient quantities of the relevant glazes (see pages 54-61), and marble one technique at a time. Work systematically round the panels, whether you are working directly on the wall or on a demountable system. Whilst you are waiting for glazes to dry on a panel, you could be scumbling the ground on the next one.

Constantly stand back and view your work from a distance, in order to ascertain the overall effect. When you have

design. They need show only the most prominent detail, and they take only minutes to prepare. Stand back and view your efforts from a distance to assess the overall effect.

Using 'book ends'

When a block of marble is cut into thin laminate panels, a similar, but slightly progressive, pattern appears in each

The centre point of a room is at the intersection of the diagonals. Fix one end of a length of string there and measure out the same distance along each diagonal, marking the end point. Join up these four points to form your squared perimeter.

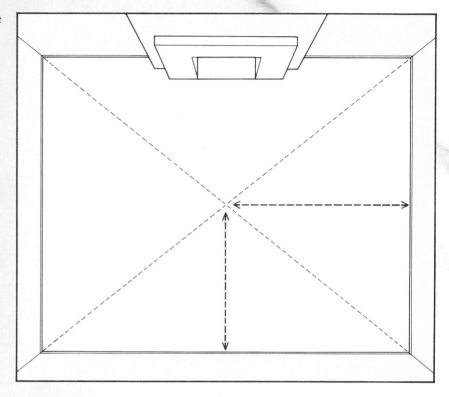

completed the entire section, and the paint has hardened off, it is advisable to detail the panel pin-supports, if these are to be included as a part of the overall design.

Direct system

When working directly on the wall, clean up the edges of your panels by outlining the joints, using a straight edge and a felt-tipped marker pen. When the whole area has been marbled, allow the finish to dry and then apply a coat of varnish, in a continuous film, working in vertical strips approximately 20 cm (8 in) in width. Make sure you keep a wet edge.

Demountable system – mounting the panels

Before mounting the panels scrub the backs with water, and allow them to stand overnight in the room where

they are to be mounted. This will avoid cracking and warping later on.

Panel mounting points should be considered as a visual feature on the panel. They may be clearly stated as screw heads or cup washers, for example; or they may be disguised by using countersunk screws and filling and touching up afterwards.

Guidelines must be accurately marked out on the walls of the room, prior to mounting the panels. The vertical accent is all important, so use a plumb line and spirit level at all panel junctions. Start from the centre of the wall and mount the panels working outwards, securing the the top edge of each panel first. If the wall is reasonably true, the panels can be screwed directly on to the wall, using rawl plugs and wood screws. If it is a lathe and plaster wall, you will first need to locate the vertical studs as fixing points. If the wall surface is irregular, the panels must be mounted on a frame system that has been squared relative to the wall surface. This is a job for a professional carpenter.

The paper alternative

As an alternative to hardboard, panels may be constructed on lining paper. After the marbling has been completed, they may be hung on the wall in much the same manner as wallpaper. While the width of the lining paper dictates the maximum size of the panels, this method is a cheaper alternative to the hardboard system, but is only possible if the wall is in very good condition.

FLOOR PANEL SYSTEMS

Although floor areas are visually less critical than walls, the impact of the geometric pattern ensures that marbled floors always attain the status of a 'feature' (see page 37).

Preparations are much the same as for walls, and involve transferring accurate dimensions of the room on to graph paper; this time incorporating on the plan such items as the door openings, furniture, fireplace and recesses. The fireplace is often the focus of the room and may be used as the starting point or lynch-pin of your design. However, the overall theme will generally be governed by the size of large items of furniture within the room. There is little point in spending time marbling a floor if most of it is to remain hidden.

Like walls, floors are rarely square. To prepare an accurate plan, first find the intersection of the diagonals. That point is the centre of the room. Fix one end of a length of string there, and measure out the same distance along each diagonal, marking the end point.

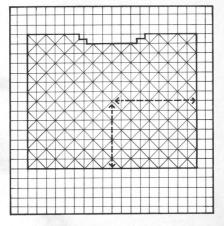

Transfer the floor measurements on to graph paper. Incorporate on your plan such items as the door openings, fireplace and recesses. Use tracing overlays to plan your panel system.

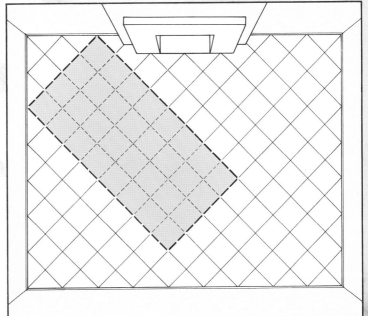

Join up these four points to form your squared perimeter.

Transfer the measurements on to graph paper and once more, using tracing overlays, construct the outlines of a panel system.

There are many traditional designs that you can copy. For example, whilst a Palladian floor design may look very

Scale-up your graph paper diagram to construct the outline of a panel system on the floor. You must accurately translate your pattern on to the floor area using chalk to mark out the lines.

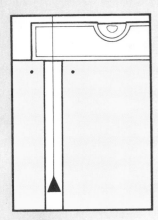

With panels, the vertical accent is all important. To make sure that the panels are straight use a plumb line and spirit level at all panel junctions.

complicated, it is only a refinement of a very simple technique. The main requisite is that you must accurately translate your pattern on to the floor area. After that it is very much a case of systematic painting by numbers. Although squared patterns are generally employed, there is no restriction on using curves, circles, ellipses or even total abstracts. These can often be used to give a room a 30s feel.

Where alcoves or recesses occur, such as either side of the fireplace, marbled panels may be carried into these areas, provided they can be represented as complete units. To do otherwise would look odd.

The outer perimeter should always be bounded by a border, which may be constructed in flat paint or a contrasting marbled theme. This too may be represented as panelling, and should be thought of as a cushion area to absorb any dimensional discrepancies that may occur in your layout or technique.

Transferring the design – the direct system

When you are happy with the outline of your plan, scale up the dimensions and redraft them on to a floor area that has already been prepared to take colour (see pages 80-2).

Transferring the design – the demountable system

If you are using a demountable system you should follow the same procedure as outlined for demountable wall panels (see page 87). The only difference, at this stage, is that you will require 6 mm (¼ in) thick board.

Composing the panels

You should adopt a similar approach to that for the composition of wall panels (see pages 86-90), but concentrate your efforts on getting the right colour strengths and contrasts between individual panels, rather than on the construction of fine details. Where a light, unicoloured floor is prepared, its geometric strength may be emphasised by accentuating the panel joints in a dark, flat paint. Veining should not be overstated in terms of colour contrast with the background.

Prepare samples and look at them on the floor, rather than on a table. It is amazing how less reflective colour is at ground level. Many layers of polyurethane varnish will be required to protect the finish, and whilst gloss textures will provide reflection, this inevitably reduces colour intensity.

Marbling the panels

When the outlines of the panel have been marked up, in chalk, on the prepared surface, mark out the main characteristics of each panel. Prepare the relevant glazes in sufficient quantities for a session. Usually, you will be marbling two, or possibly three different techniques at the same time, so organise the creation of the glazes on separate palettes.

Direct system

When you are working directly on the surface of the floor, rather than on a demountable system, begin marbling at the perimeter of the room. Work in parallel bands, and be careful not to box yourself in – you should always work towards an exit.

When the design is complete, and the paint dry, use a thick felt pen and a straight edge to correct or accentuate panel junctions.

Varnish the floor with the recommended number of coats, and use a soft fabric kneeling pad to prevent damage to the decorative surface.

Many of the time problems associated with painting floors can be overcome by using floor paint or liquid lino (an oil-based paint that has been specially formulated to cover wood or cement surfaces). It has good covering capacity, requiring a maximum of two coats, is extremely tough and does not require varnishing. The drawbacks are that it comes in a limited colour range, and dries to a dull, rubbery film. Although special colours may be made by intermixing, the addition of concentrated pigments is not recommended. For those who require bold patterns and little sophistication, it is an ideal choice for heavily used areas, such as hallways, bathrooms and kitchens, which cannot be out of commission for too long.

Demountable system

The problems of drying time point to the great advantage of the demountable system. With marbled floors requiring up to six coats of polyurethane varnish to protect the finish, when using the direct system the room can be out of action for over a week. However, the demountable system allows you to varnish the panels off-site, before fixing in place.

The technique for mounting the panels is very similar to that employed for mounting wall panel systems (see page 90).

PANELLING ON FURNITURE

Large items of furniture, such as a chest of drawers or a table top, can be marbled using a simple direct panel system. Starting with a small scale project such as this will reveal many of the problems that you are likely to encounter later on when tackling more ambitious marbling schemes.

Direct system

Once again, scale drawings are useful. When you have identified your panel design, cut out the various sections in paper (possibly painted out in the predominant colour of your marbling technique), and lay or stick them on to the surface to get an impression of the overall effect.

Draw out your design on a previously applied ground coat (see page 99), and indicate the technique to be employed in each area.

When working on this scale, you have the opportunity to concentrate on detailed marbling, so try for a truly authentic finish. Inlay work featuring precious stones such as malachite (see page 116) can be most effective. As a contrast, feature them against panels displaying reflective foils, iridescent surfaces or mother of pearl inlay. Patterns may be used to accentuate the geometry of the piece. On this scale, sharp contrasts can add visual weight without becoming strident.

This type of work is also a great opportunity to test your varnishing skills, thus indicating the surface qualities of individual stones.

Demountable system

As an alternative, for small scale panelling systems, a plastic film with an adhesive backing (available from most stationers) provides an excellent surface on which to marble. Use it as a means of creating a small inlay system – on a table top, for example. Cut out the panels, give them individual treatments, remove the protective backing and stick them on to the table top. Be careful to transfer them accurately to the surface, following the prescribed design, because the material is exceptionally sticky and you will only have one chance to get it right.

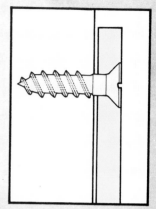

If you wish to disguise the panel mounting points use countersunk screws, overfill and touch-up afterwards.

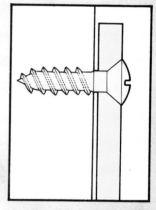

Panels may be mounted using screw heads or cap washers and, as the heads are to feature as part of the design, these should be painted too.

7

STARTING TO MARBLE

The aim of this chapter is to show the beginner how to simulate marble, step-by-step. The chapter starts with a description of the qualities of marble that need to be understood before embarking on a painted illusion. This is followed by detailed instructions on rendering a selection of popular marbles. Once you have studied this chapter and mastered the skills in Chapter Four: Broken Colour Techniques, you should be able to copy virtually any marble in paint.

UNDERSTANDING THE ILLUSION

The tremendous variety in the appearance of polished marble is mainly a product of two interdependent factors: the various permutations of different colours; and certain abstract qualities, such as solidity, translucency, depth, cloudiness and motion. These are present in all marbles, to a greater or lesser degree. In order to make the most of your painted illusion you must identify and examine these features in order to see what each contributes to the overall appearance of the material you are trying to copy.

Colour

Fundamental to our appreciation and understanding of the material world, colour is a vital ingredient in the process of communication and expression. In the home, colour is the most import-

ant ingredient in a design scheme: it can define space, indicate function, influence mood and even project personality.

The qualities of colour include temperature – warm and cold hues; and sound – quiet colours, colours that shout or jangle, resonant colours and harmonising colours. Colour also has distance – advancing and retreating colours; and mood – we regard some colours as happy and expansive, others as mournful and sombre. Colour even affects time; it appears to pass faster in brightly coloured rooms. It is a knowledge of these qualities that provides us with a blueprint for our selection and use of colour. Broadly, colours can be categorised as follows:

☐ Yellow-greens and red-browns, by reminding us of a bountiful earth, are reassuring and restful.

☐ Orange-reds, by reflecting the sun,

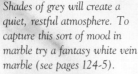

Shades of grey will create a quiet, restful atmosphere. To capture this sort of mood in marble try a fantasy white vein marble (see pages 124-5).

Light, bright yellows, like a sunny day, create a cheerful mood. To produce such a look in marble, try yellow onyx (see page 119).

the source of life, are warm and vibrant.

☐ Blue-greens, echoing the sea, can be cool and inviting, or mysterious and forbidding.

☐ Grey-blues and red-purples, in their ever-changing gradations, remind us of the sky, and convey distance and depth.

☐ Dark greys and black, like the night, are enclosing and restful or forbidding.

☐ Lighter colours, like daytime, are optimistic and expansive.

To illustrate how you can use these qualities to your advantage, look at the problems encountered when decorating a cramped space or room. The standard response is to paint the walls and ceiling white. While this may relieve the feeling of claustrophobia, the room can often feel oppressive if

Red-brown colours are reminiscent of the earth, and so give a warm, restful impression. To render this sort of scheme in marble, try rojo alicante (see page 108).

the room has a southerly aspect – white reflects bright sunlight, and this combination can visually roast the occupants. However, if the white is tinted with the merest hint of blue, the surfaces will be cooled without destroying the illusion of space. Conversely, north-facing rooms that appear chilly on all but the brightest days, may be warmed with the addition of a pale yellow-orange.

So, before marbling any surface, whether it be an entire wall or a fire surround, think carefully about the effect of the colour you are going to use. It is irritating, to say the least, to embark on a detailed scheme only to discover half way through that the effect is, for

example, too heavy and overbearing. Where there are large areas to be marbled, it is particularly important to get the predominant colour right. When you have selected colours, paint out small samples and position them in the room where they are to be used, live with them a little, view them in natural and artificial light, and see how they combine with other surfaces and textures in the room. Get the consensus of opinion from other members of the family. They will have to live with it, as well as you.

Finally, do remember that few of us begin with a blank canvas. That is, some consideration must also be given to the manner in which permanent fixtures and fittings tint and tone any colours that we may select.

Solidity

Marble is a stone of great mass. Whilst your marbled surface must always reflect this feature, the painted illusion should also convey the fact that different marbles present varying degrees of solidity. The black or dark green marbles, and those whose surfaces exhibit tight, regular patterns in contrasting opaques, such as the granites or the porphyries, are capable of implying a monumental solidity.

On the other hand, the pale, unicoloured or variegated marbles with little or no pattern suggest a lightness and airiness that totally betrays their mass. This latter quality is admirably demonstrated in the classical statues of antiquity. Executed in pure white Carrara marble, these elegant figures appear to float, apparently weightless, in the atmosphere.

It is important to bear these factors in mind when choosing a particular stone to copy. Some marbles will prove overbearing in a particular room, and others will lack presence.

Translucency

A feature exhibited by many of the pale, unicoloured or variegated marbles, translucency is typified by an inner glow, which appears to emanate from within the body of the stone, and produces a feeling of lightness and space. The effect is easily simulated by applying transparent, coloured glazes over pale or white grounds (see page 61). This marbled effect gives a sense of space in cramped areas.

The darker coloured marble illusions may also show a degree of translucency, if established by the application of a light opaque colour over a satin black

ground. These contrasting layers seem to hang in the mid-ground like some vast, frozen, illuminated network. This effect, when given a highly reflective gloss finish, is particularly suitable for simulating a marble table top.

Cloudiness

This is a quality typified by smoky, imprecise veils of colour that appear trapped within the body of the stone. The effect is readily simulated by 'ragging' or 'sponging' (see page 65). Painted on a surface, a cloudy illusion will always imply mystery and depth – qualities that can be very useful in areas where atmospheric lighting is required.

Depth

The impression of depth can be readily suggested by overlaying prominent elements, such as veining patterns or strata formations, one upon the other (see page 73). Constructed on a cloudy backdrop, these elements appear to float imprecisely within veils of frozen colour, and the illusion of depth is further enhanced. This feature is very useful for creating a feeling of space within a room.

Motion

Veined patterns suggest direction and motion. For the interior designer, this is perhaps the most versatile quality that marbling can capture. An impression of space can be varied by the manner in which the pattern of the selected marble may hold or direct the eye over a surface. For example, tightly patterned marbles appear static and solid; whereas those which exhibit subtle gradations of banded strata, that meander casually over the surface, imply movement and space – the latter being an important illusion in these days of small-roomed dwellings.

Marble sequences
The detailed simulations of marbles shown on the following pages were carried out on 3 mm (⅛ in) hardboard sheeting. The shiny surface provides a cheap and practical practice area. However, it is necessary to construct a mid-sheen ground in white eggshell before applying the coloured glazes.

Constructing the eggshell ground
1 Ensure that the hardboard panel is clean, dry and free of oil or grease.
2 Using a 6 cm (2½ in) brush, apply a sufficient number of coats of white oil-based undercoat to cover the natural colour of the hardboard (two coats is generally enough). Leave for 24 hours to dry.
3 Lightly abrade with medium grade sandpaper. Remove any dust with a clean cloth.
4 Using the same brush, apply two coats of white eggshell paint. Allow the surface to harden off for 24 hours.
5 Lightly abrade the surface with fine grade sandpaper.
6 Immediately before marbling, wipe the surface over with a 'tac-rag' or a cloth moistened with white spirit to remove the last traces of dust.

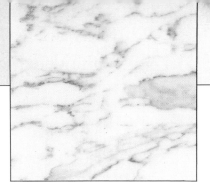

White Vein Marble

White Vein is the archetypal marble, and occurs in abundance throughout the world. It is a predominantly white, translucent and semi-lustrous stone that exhibits an irregular veining pattern, featured against a white, mottled ground.

The grey veins show green, blue or yellow tonal discolorations, and strike out over the ground collectively, in one direction. Many types are very understated. The veins are dislocated or non-continuous, and appear to move in vague, broken, blurred parallels deep within the stone. The pattern density varies enormously, but the more decorative varieties tend to exhibit a sparse, but clearly stated forked design.

The overall effect is one of subtlety, with the characteristic depth being occasionally and surprisingly interrupted by pale pink or green pastel veils, which appear to hang in the mid-ground.

Occasionally, opaque white imperfections sit on the surface and obscure the crystalline structure. Also, dark opaque faults occur where veins break the surface.

The stone is generally exhibited with the veining pattern describing the characteristic diagonal accent. 'Book end' patterning is used when the veining is clearly stated.

The numerous ways of simulating this marble demonstrates the range of options open to the marbler, and the importance of developing your own style and approach. Sketches,

photographs or an actual example of the marble will prove invaluable for reference.

The simulation may be applied to any and all surfaces, provided the pattern does not become too overstated. Where prominent patterns are depicted, the stone is generally found on featured objects such as fireplaces, table tops, or as a wall-cladding material with prominent veins featured in formal, diagonal patterning.

Provided ground colours remain translucent, any number of fantasies can be constructed by scumbling and veining the ground in two or three different shades of the same colour.

MATERIALS

White oil-based eggshell
Artists' oils: Payne's grey, yellow ochre, raw umber
Transparent oil glaze (scumble glaze)
White (mineral) spirit
Polyurethane varnish
Clean, lint-free cloth
Hog's hair softening brushes (medium and small)
Artists' brushes (medium and fine)
Three poor quality 4 cm (1.5 in) flat brushes (with splayed bristles)
Varnishing brush

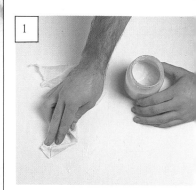

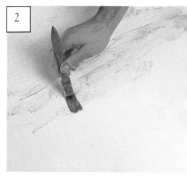

1 *Wipe a thin layer of neat scumble glaze over the entire surface of the prepared white eggshell ground, using a clean cloth.*

2 *Mix three transparent, tonal grey glazes on the palette by blending varying proportions of raw umber, Payne's grey and yellow ochre with white spirit. The glazes should be very transparent so that they merely dirty or discolour the ground. Working systematically over the panel, apply the prepared glazes in loose, irregular squiggles, using the flat brushes in a casual stippling and dabbing action. Using a separate brush for each glaze, attempt to strike a predominantly diagonal accent in the ground.*

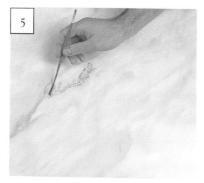

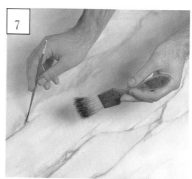

3 Continue applying the glazes in this fashion to the entire panel, but leave plenty of the white background showing through. Avoid overlapping the glazes, and remember that the darker areas will serve to indicate the path of the major veins, and thus the form of the final composition. In this respect it is important to work to a rough sketch or design.

4 Using a hog's hair softener, soften and blend the colours by gently pulling the dry bristles of the brush through the wet glazes in all directions. However, emphasise the directional flow in the ground by concentrating more on a diagonal accent with the brush, but do adjust the pressure and its direction to accentuate any promising features. If any areas appear overstated or too colourful, they may be wiped out with a cloth and softened. Areas that appear weak may be strengthened by stippling on more glaze. Featherlight finishing strokes with the softening brush will disguise any obvious brush marks.

5 Secondary veins are now introduced in a mid-tone transparent grey, prepared by blending Payne's grey and raw umber with white spirit and a little scumble glaze. The veins trace out roughly diagonal paths, and accentuate the darker channels in the ground. Using a medium artists' brush, fidget the veins onto the surface with a casual, imprecise, dithering action.

6 The secondary veins that lie beneath the surface must appear as little more than shadows. Therefore, immediately they are painted in, they must be softened by pulling a softening and blending brush along the length of a vein, and also at right angles to its directional flow. Then, referring to the sketch of your design, paint-in and soften the remaining secondary veins that appear on the surface. Now allow the panel to dry overnight.

7 After once more applying a thin layer of scumble glaze to the ground, the primary veins are painted in; their course roughly follows and reinforces the direction of the secondary veins. Use a fine artists' brush to apply the glaze, which is a slightly more opaque version of that used for the secondary veins. Again, it will be necessary to lightly soften all but the finest veins. Use a small hog's hair softener to achieve the most subtle and effective results.

8 After the completed panel has dried out, apply two coats of mid-sheen polyurethane varnish. This not only affords a degree of protection, but also imitates the lustrous, rather than reflective qualities of white vein marble.

Black and Gold Marble

In complete contrast to the tonal nuances of White Vein (see pages 100-1), Black and Gold marble (commercially named Portoro) exhibits a bold, yellow-gold veining pattern contrasted against a satin-black, opaque ground. The surface is always highly polished and reflective, contributing to an overall impression of sophistication and opulence.

On wall surfaces the veins of this marble are traditionally featured as vertical elements that hang in loosely interlinked, chain-like formations. The only additional element to the abstract simplicity of this pattern is a white mist, which hangs and swirls in the mid-ground, like the cloudy veils of cigarette smoke. Many people feel this feature to be an unnecessary distraction to the spectacular veining system, and therefore will omit it from the simulation.

The apparent simplicity of the veining pattern is deceptive. There is great subtlety in the structural formation and the visual weight of the various elements. Consequently, it requires a careful examination of the natural stone, and a good deal of practice, to capture an authentic simulation. The veining structure and additional details take some time to reproduce. So, it is only practical to carry out the work in the relatively slow drying, oil-based paints. However, the basic method is fairly straightforward, and the potential for fantasy applications is limitless.

Because of its sumptuous, sophisticated and atmospheric qualities,

Black and Gold should be used in areas that are appropriate to such style. Wall surfaces in bathrooms and bedrooms are favourites; although in a living room the effect can be very moody. Table tops, obelisks and ornament bases are also popular subjects for this treatment.

For a variation, look at a piece of St. Annes' marble, which is similar to Portoro, but with a more uniform veining pattern.

MATERIALS

Black oil-based eggshell
Artists' oils: white, yellow ochre, burnt Sienna, raw umber
Scumble glaze (flatting oil)
White (mineral) spirit
White polish
Polyurethane varnish (gloss)
Rubbing compound
Aerosol wax
2.5 cm (1 in) standard flat brush
Artists' brush (fine)
Hog's hair softening brushes (medium and fine)
Varnishing brush
Stiff bristled mop (small)
Clean, lint-free cloth
Pencil eraser
Polishing cloth
Fine grade sandpaper

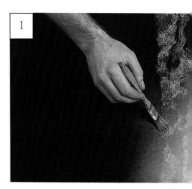

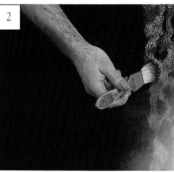

1 *Wipe a thin layer of neat scumble glaze over the surface of a black eggshell ground, using a clean cloth. Then, prepare a yellow-gold glaze by blending yellow ochre, white, burnt Sienna and raw umber with white spirit. With the flat brush loosely stipple the glaze onto the panel, in the rough shape of the first veining chain. Because the chains are intricate and time consuming to construct, work on only one vein at a time.*

2 *Immediately soften and blend the glaze into an approximation of the finished vein, using a hog's hair softener.*

3 *Use a pencil eraser (with its edges cut clean by a craft knife) to wipe out or displace sections of the glaze, and reinforce the definitive chain-like signature of the marble. Start with the insides of the vein and finish with the outer edges, working in a continuous movement down the length of the panel.*

4 *The procedure is exactly the same for each chain; but note the thin, horizontal filaments that link them. They too are created by displacing and wiping out the glaze with a pencil eraser.*

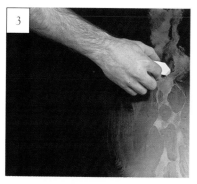

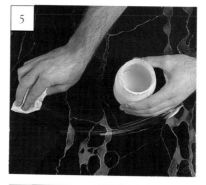

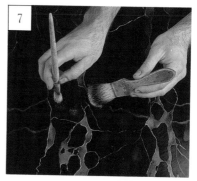

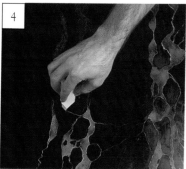

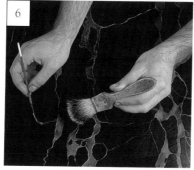

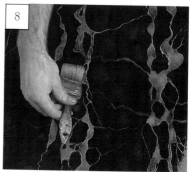

5 After the panel has been allowed to dry overnight, apply a thin layer of scumble glaze to the surface.

6 The secondary veins appear to lie well beneath the polished surface of the natural stone. They are ghost images of the major veining chains, and the sinewy elements that link them. Detail them with a fine artists' brush, using a transparent white glaze prepared by blending white artists' oil with white spirit. Immediately soften using a small hog's hair brush.

7 Ghost images of the chain elements appear as loose, ovoid fossil forms. They nestle in the inner recesses, and cling to the outer edges, of the chains. Detail them, with the same transparent white glaze as in step 6, by softly stippling onto the panel in small, irregular patches, using a stiff-bristled mop. Immediately soften with the small softening brush, and leave to dry.

8 The panel now exhibits the primary veining system and the secondary ghost images. It is important that the latter should not have been overstated, if the subtle finish of this marble is to be captured.

9 The wiping out process in steps 3 and 4 leaves prominent ridges and high spots on the surface. To level it, apply four coats of white polish, in quick succession. When dry, lightly abrade with fine grade sandpaper. After removing all traces of dust, apply one or two coats of gloss polyurethane varnish.

10 Finally, the surface may be polished with a fine rubbing compound, and finished off with a domestic aerosol furniture wax.

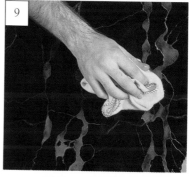

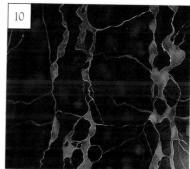

Sienna Marble

'Sienna marble' originally described a specific variety of rock quarried in and around the province of Sienna. However, the name is now applied to any stone that exhibits a predominantly yellow, variegated ground, that is crossed and sectioned in the foreground by a random, darkly stated, sinewy veining pattern.

The marble is partially translucent, and the background appears as irregular patches of colour, which range from white, through pale creams to strong yellow-ochres and red-browns.

Some areas look fractured, and their appearance, which may be rounded or angular, is gently outlined and strengthened, to form a softly-stated network. A directional flow is suggested in the shape of these sections as they become grouped and enclosed within a more powerfully stated veining system. Darker lines, that begin as fine, spidery elements, join them to form concentrated and strongly defined branching networks, which eventually unite at the major veining nodes. At these dominant intersections, small ovals of entrapped colour cling to the branching veins like precious stones around a necklace.

Where major veins breach the surface, their images cloud into ragged and blurred shadows. Travelling on across the ground the veins once more disperse, fade and are eventually lost in the quilted ground.

'Sienna' is an exellent example of a 'balanced' marble. When simulated, it is one in which the superimposed veining may be controlled to counterbalance the underlying colour strength of the ground. In this respect it is extremely forgiving, and may be applied to wall surfaces throughout the home.

The colours are warm and sunny, and therefore the marble is ideal for establishing continuity and atmosphere in dowdy areas, such as halls and stairwells.

MATERIALS

White oil-based eggshell
Artists' oils: burnt Sienna,
Davies grey, yellow ochre,
ultramarine, Indian red, raw
umber
Scumble glaze (flatting oil)
White (mineral) spirit
Polyurethane varnish (mid-sheen)
Hog's hair softening brushes (medium and small)
Artists' brush (fine)
4 cm (1½ in) flat brush (of poor quality with splayed bristles)
Cellophane (or some other crisp, non-absorbent paper)
Cotton buds (Q-tips)
Varnishing brush

1 *Prepare a strong yellow glaze by combining yellow ochre with small quantities of Davies grey, burnt Sienna and white spirit. Thin it to transparency and combine it with a little scumble glaze Then use the flat brush to apply it loosely onto the prepared white eggshell panel into irregular shapes, using a photograph or sketch of the marble for reference.*

2 *Prepare a pale yellow-grey glaze, by toning down the glaze produced in stage 1 with Davies Grey. Thin it to transparency, blend in a little scumble glaze and apply it to the remaining white areas of the panel, using a loose dabbing and stippling action.*

3 *Although the scumbled panel is now completely covered with colour, the thinned glazes allow much of the white ground to show through.*

4 *Blend and merge the colours by striking the panel in all directions, using a hog's hair softener.*

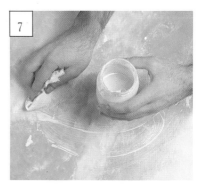

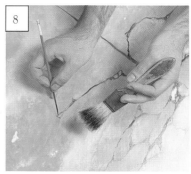

5 Using a piece of cellophane held in a loose ball, distress the surface with a light stippling and rolling action. The colours will merge and be slightly displaced, to reveal small sections of the ground. Working systematically over the panel, immediately soften the distressed areas with a softening brush to produce the characteristic bruised appearance of Sienna marble.

6 Using a cotton bud, wipe out small sections of the glaze back to the white ground. The positioning of these areas is important to the overall design, as they are on the paths taken by the major veins, and they feature in the finished simulation as small fossil forms.

7 After the panel has dried overnight, apply a thin layer of scumble glaze to the entire surface, using a cloth.

8 To establish the primary veins, first prepare a glaze by combining ultramarine, Indian red and raw umber with white spirit and a little scumble glaze. Apply it with a fine artists' brush, using a dithering, imprecise movement – rolling and spreading the bristles of the brush to produce a variable signature. Use a small softener to blur those veins which appear overstated.

Note how the primary veins tend to feature more strongly in the darker areas of the panel. They strike a roughly diagonal accent, splitting and recombining to enclose and emphasise areas of colour and detail in the coloured ground.

9 To apply the secondary veins, first mix a paler version of the glaze used in step 8. Again, apply it with a fine artists' brush, and immediately soften it with a small softening brush. Note how these veins are ghost images of the major veins, and appear as a pale matrix that lies well beneath the surface. They occupy and enclose features in the lighter parts of the ground, and in some cases link the primary veins.

10 When the panel is dry apply one or two coats of mid-sheen polyurethane varnish both for protection, and to provide a lustrous finish.

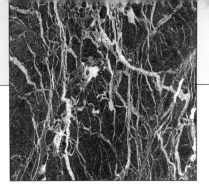

Red Levanto

One of the most highly prized and decorative varieties of Breccia marble is Ophicalcite or 'Red Levanto'. The Breccia marbles are classified as sedimentary, and identified as stones or fractured, angular, rock sections frozen in a fine, solidified matrix of lime and cement (containing calcite or quartz). This complex network may be likened to some vast abstract jigsaw, an intricate road map or even the familiar crazy paving of our paths and patios.

Despite the tremendous variation of colour and form in the polished surface, the techniques for capturing these characteristics in paint are relatively simple.

Because Red Levanto is essentially a dark marble, extensive use on wall areas should be restricted to all but the largest interiors. However, it presents a 'busy' surface that commands close inspection. Consequently, isolated panels may be prepared as features within a room.

Red Levanto is used extensively for contrasting borders to paler coloured marbles. And its application to furniture is restricted to items such as table tops, bath surrounds or shelves, where its presence always suggests formality, weight and mass.

MATERIALS
**White oil-based eggshell
Artists' oils: white, alizarin crimson, veridian, Indian red, Payne's grey
Scumble glaze (flatting oil)
White (mineral) spirit
White polish
Polyurethane varnish
Hog's hair softening brushes
4 cm (1½ in) and 2.5 cm (1 in) standard flat brushes
Artists' brushes (medium and fine)
Artists' palette and dippers
Cellophane (or similar crisp and non-absorbent material)
Pencil eraser
Cotton buds (Q-tips)
Fine grade sandpaper
Varnishing brush
Polishing cloth**

1 *After applying scumble to the eggshell ground, prepare a deep red glaze by blending Alizarin crimson and Indian red with small quantities of veridian green and Payne's grey. Add sufficient white spirit to produce a degree of transparency, and then brush the glaze onto the panel with a 4 cm (1½ in) brush, using a casual dabbing and stippling action. Refer to a sketch to ascertain the distribution of the colour in the scumbled ground, as this determines the position of the superimposed veining detail.*

2 *Prepare a dark green glaze by blending veridian with the glaze produced in stage 1. Apply this to the white areas of the panel, but allow more of the ground to show through. Establish tonal variations in the established red ground by dabbing on isolated patches of the green glaze.*

3 *Soften the tonal gradations of colour between the red and green areas using a hog's hair softening brush.*

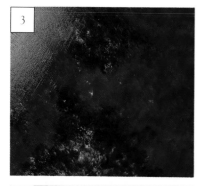

4 Now work irregular patches of a transparent glaze of Payne's grey onto the red areas, using a brush, and soften it to produce depth and tonal variations in the ground.

5 Using a piece of cellophane held in a loose ball, distress the red areas of the panel. The glaze will be wiped out or displaced, to reveal sections of the ground. A light softening will produce further tonal variations.

6 Using a cotton bud, wipe out small, angular sections of the glaze to reveal the ground, and introduce a transparent veridian green glaze into them, using a medium artists' brush. These softened sections will appear as translucent highlights in the final composition.

7 When dry, apply a thin layer of scumble glaze to the whole surface. Then prepare a transparent white wash by blending white artists' oil with white spirit, and stipple it onto those areas that are to carry the major veining system. Soften immediately.

8 Using the flat edge of a pencil eraser, displace colour to expose interesting angular and ovoid sections in the scumbled ground. By angling the eraser, create pronounced ridges which will establish the network of the major veins. Use the same technique to harden off the outer rims of the white glaze to a clean edge.

9 The major veining system is highlighted by consolidating sections of the ridged, white network that strikes across the panel. Use a more opaque white glaze, and stiffen it slightly with a little scumble. Apply it using a fine or medium artists' brush, and soften the veins immediately so that they are not overstated.

10 Level off the surface relief and irregularities, caused by the displacing and wiping-out techniques, by applying five or six coats of white polish. When hardened, abrade it with fine sandpaper. Finally, apply two coats of gloss polyurethane varnish.

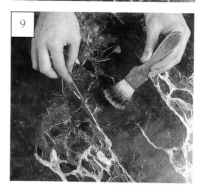

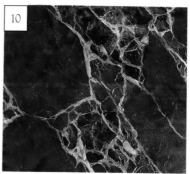

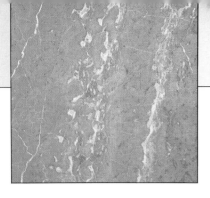

Rojo Alicante

Although this type of marble occurs in a variety of forms, its surface is generally expressed as a predominantly red ground covered by roughly parallel, chain-like veining. The veins, which look like strips of torn cloth blowing in a breeze, follow vague channels that appear in the loosely stratified ground.

The variegated reds of the ground are mottled with grey-green, and the entire surface is crossed and recrossed by fine, white fracture lines, which link the main veining structures. The lighter tones of green appear to follow the main veining chains, whilst the darker tones of green are spotted unevenly over the surface.

Generally, the marble is pleasingly understated, and projects a warm rosy glow in any interior where it is employed. The scale of the dominant veining repeat is only evident when applied over quite large areas. Consequently, the simulation is most successfully employed as a panel system (see pages 86-90) on wall surfaces. Marbled panels are cut and displayed in such a manner that the veining elements are presented as near vertical accents. A slight inclination adds a certain tension to the panel.

MATERIALS
White oil-based eggshell
Artists' oils: white, burnt Sienna, burnt umber, Davies grey, yellow ochre
Scumble glaze (flatting oil)
White (mineral) spirit
Oil-based crayon (black)
Polyurethane varnish (mid-sheen)
2.5 cm (1 in) standard flat brush
Hog's hair softening brush
Artists' brush (medium to fine)
Natural marine sponge
Clean, lint-free cloth
Cotton buds (Q-tips)
Varnishing brush

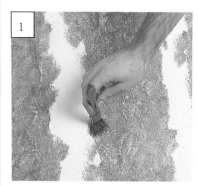

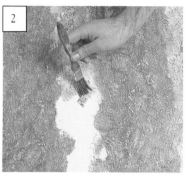

1 Prepare a reddy-brown glaze by blending burnt umber, burnt Sienna, white and Davies grey with white spirit and scumble. Using a flat brush, loosely stipple and dab the glaze onto the prepared white eggshell panel to create broad bands of colour. The channels that remain will carry the major, chain-like veining system.

2 Prepare a pale, yellow-brown glaze by tinting a transparent glaze of Davies grey with small amounts of the glaze produced in stage 1. Use a loose, stippling action to dab the colour into the white channels, and roughly merge it into the reddy-brown areas.

3 Immediately, blend the different glazes together by striking the surface of the panel, in all directions, with a hog's hair softening brush. The tonal variations in the applied glazes and the ragged channels will now be clearly evident in the scumbled ground.

4 Secondary veins in the darker areas of the marble are now introduced onto the ground. Using a cotton bud soaked in white spirit, pull through the wet

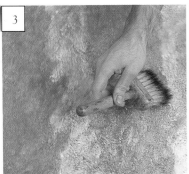

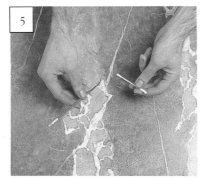

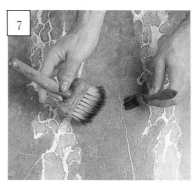

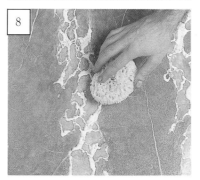

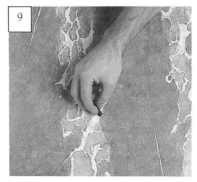

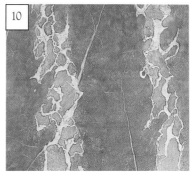

glaze to ciss or open up the colour and reveal the white ground. Lightly soften the edges with the hog's hair brush.

5 The primary veins are now added to the lighter channels. They are created one at a time, working from the top to the bottom of the panel. Load a fine artists' brush with white spirit and, as with the cotton bud in step 4, pull it through the wet glaze to open up the colour and reveal the white ground. Varying the pressure on the bristles, and angling the brush will ensure the necessary variation in width of the small veins. Use a cotton bud to control the cissing action by mopping up excess white spirit.

6 Having allowed the panel to dry overnight, apply a thin layer of scumble glaze to the entire surface.

7 Prepare a thin, pale yellow-grey glaze by blending yellow ochre, Davies grey and white with white spirit and a little scumble glaze. Stipple and dab the glaze onto the red areas in the scumbled ground, and immediately soften it with a hog's hair softener.

8 Lightly dab a natural marine sponge, moistened with white spirit, onto the yellow-grey glaze. The cissed colour will open to reveal small, irregular patches in the red ground, and in so doing will produce the delicate, veil-like quality of the marble finish.

9 After the panel has dried overnight, use a black, oil-based crayon to outline and visually advance some of the interesting details in the primary veining system. Moisten the tip of the crayon with white spirit, and work systematically down the veins. Take care not to overdo it, or the subtlety of the finish will be lost.

10 When the surface is dry, apply a coat of mid-sheen polyurethane varnish, both for protection and to give the surface a lustrous appearance.

Breche Violet

The popularity of Breche Violet is largely accounted for by the fact that it exhibits many of the truly classical features of polished stone. Angular and ovoid fragments of rock, of a predominantly red-purple-violet hue, are grouped together, and enclosed within a powerfully stated veining system that meanders unpredictably over a variegated, pale and translucent ground.

Whilst the marble is cherished for its forthright and honest simplicity, there is a certain subtle contradiction implied in the surface. Viewed from a distance, the veining system can sometimes appear as some vast abstract necklace, with the coloured fragments hanging like transparent jewels against the illuminated backdrop of what appears to be silk, or even skin.

Large deposits have ensured a tremendous range and scale of pattern repeats. This variety ensures that the simulation has many applications: the marble itself is equally at home in a fireplace or the pillars of the Victoria and Albert museum.

While the marble may be simulated equally well in both the oil and water-based systems, there is a certain ethereal quality implied in the stone which is more readily captured by the matt finish qualities of water-based paints.

You will find that it is most important to work from a prepared sketch, photograph or sample; the veining patterns, which appear random and loose, are in fact deceptively hard to capture.

MATERIALS
White oil-based eggshell
Artists' oils: yellow ochre,
Payne's grey, ultramarine,
Indian red, crimson
Scumble glaze (flatting oil)
White (mineral) spirit
White polish
Polyurethane varnish (mid-sheen)
2.5 cm (1 in) standard flat brush
Hog's hair softening brushes
Artists' brushes
Clean, lint-free cloth
Pencil eraser
Fine grade sandpaper
Varnishing brush

1 Wipe a thin layer of neat scumble glaze over the surface of the white eggshell ground, using a clean cloth. Prepare a creamy yellow glaze by blending yellow ochre with small quantities of crimson, Payne's grey and white spirit. Using the flat brush, loosely stipple the glaze onto the panel, to produce a mottled pattern with a diagonal accent.

2 Soften and blend the surface in all directions, using a hog's hair brush, but try to emphasise the diagonal strokes. The tonal variations produced in the mottled ground will serve as pathways for the superimposed veins.

3 Referring to a sketch or photograph of the marble, remove angular sections of glaze, using a clean cloth. The exposed white ground will reflect light through the subsequently applied blocks of colour, and thereby simulate the characteristic translucency of the stone. Leave the panel to dry.

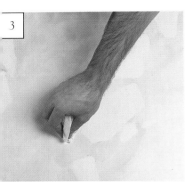

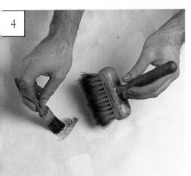

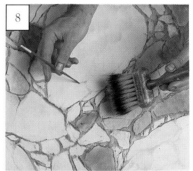

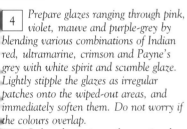

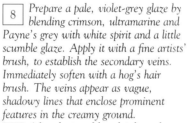

4 Prepare glazes ranging through pink, violet, mauve and purple-grey by blending various combinations of Indian red, ultramarine, crimson and Payne's grey with white spirit and scumble glaze. Lightly stipple the glazes as irregular patches onto the wiped-out areas, and immediately soften them. Do not worry if the colours overlap.

5 Soften the entire surface, using the hog's hair brush.

6 After the panel has dried, wipe a thin layer of scumble glaze over the surface. Then, prepare a transparent, purple-grey glaze by blending Indian red and Payne's grey with white spirit and a little scumble glaze. Apply the glaze to those areas of the ground that are to carry the major veins (refer to sketch or photo), and lightly soften with a hog's hair brush.

7 Using the flat edge of a pencil eraser, displace the glaze and harden up the outline of the major veins. Start within the coloured areas, and work outwards. Note that the veins do not exactly enclose individual blocks of colour.

8 Prepare a pale, violet-grey glaze by blending crimson, ultramarine and Payne's grey with white spirit and a little scumble glaze. Apply it with a fine artists' brush, to establish the secondary veins. Immediately soften with a hog's hair brush. The veins appear as vague, shadowy lines that enclose prominent features in the creamy ground.

9 After the panel has dried, apply a thin layer of scumble glaze to the major veins. Then, prepare a slightly more opaque grey-purple glaze by blending Indian red and Payne's grey with white spirit and a little scumble glaze. Apply it with a fine artists' brush, to strengthen, and give tone and depth to the major veins – but don't overdo it.

10 The displaced glaze will have produced a small amount of surface relief. So, apply three or four coats of white polish, and when it has dried, rub down with a fine, abrasive paper. Finally, apply 1 or 2 coats of mid-sheen polyurethane varnish.

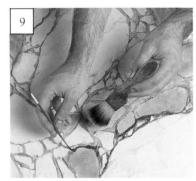

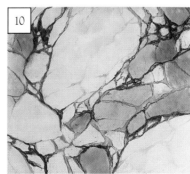

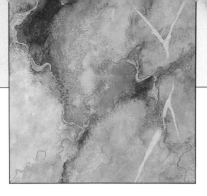

Bois Jourdan

This most elegant of marbles features irregular patches of variegated red colour, scattered over a mottled, light grey ground. However, the most striking characteristic of the stone is the unusual primary veining system, in which individual veins appear as yellow/gold, sinewy filaments. The more powerfully stated major veins follow convoluted routes through the ground, and link prominent areas of deep colour, whilst the smaller veins thread their way through the lighter, grey areas.

This system is most unusual in that it contradicts the basic pattern of many marbles; not only do isolated veins describe roughly curved patterns, but they also make a sudden appearance in the middle of the ground, and then just as suddenly disappear again. Also, where the gold veins meet the red areas, the two elements interrelate to produce distinctive, flat and angular details.

Another unusual feature of the marble is the secondary veining system. Individual veins lying close to the surface appear as white, tapered sticks. They are sparsely and irregularly scattered over the ground, and their paths bear no relationship to any underlying features. In this respect their positioning plays an important part in building up visual tension in any marbled panel.

The overall tonal value of the stone is light, with the random areas of colour and the veining systems combining to produce a marble that is both subtle and exotic, yet pleas-

ingly understated. In order to retain these essential qualities it is important to employ restraint when detailing the veining system; veins should be clearly stated, isolated and sparingly dispersed over the surfaces.

Bois Jourdan is a versatile marble, and may be applied with equal success to room surfaces and furniture. Although it can be used extensively on wall areas without the effect becoming strident, the imprecise nature and form of the veins and other features are such that it is best displayed as a featured composition within clearly stated panels.

On the other hand, you will find that a horizontal surface, such as a table top, is more forgiving, and will allow far more detail to be worked into the ground.

MATERIALS
White oil-based eggshell
Artists' oils: Payne's grey,
Indian red, yellow ochre,
raw umber
Scumble glaze (flatting oil)
White (mineral) spirit
Copper powder
Polyurethane varnish
2.5 cm (1 in) standard flat
brush
Artists' brush (fine)
Hog's hair softening brush
Cotton buds (Q-tips)
Varnishing brush

[1] *Apply a thin layer of scumble glaze to the surface of the white eggshell ground. Prepare a pale, grey-purple glaze by blending Payne's grey, raw umber and Indian red with white spirit. Thin it to transparency, and apply it with a flat brush to the ground, using a stippling and dabbing action.*

[2] *Immediately soften the glaze with hog's hair softener. Encourage any promising details, and create visual movement by working on a rough diagonal.*

[3] *Thin the glaze created in step 1, with white spirit. Apply it to select areas of the panel, using a loose stippling motion. The cissed glaze will separate to reveal the underlying colour. Immediately lightly tone down the effect with the hog's hair softener. Allow the glaze to harden for 10 minutes.*

[4] *The scumbled ground now exhibits the many tonal variations and fossil-like forms that are characteristic of the polished marble. These features determi*

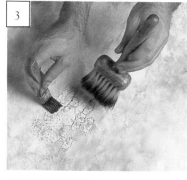

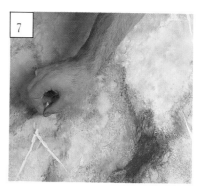

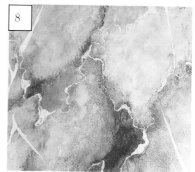

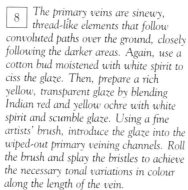

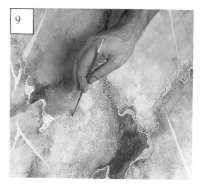

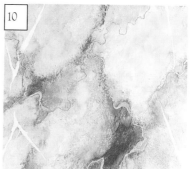

where the deeper areas of colour and the superimposed veins are positioned. It is best to work with reference to a sketch or photograph.

5 Prepare deeper tonal variations of the glaze used in step 1 by increasing the proportions of raw umber and Indian red. Apply the reddy-brown glaze to the panel, with a loose stippling action. Use the features produced when scumbling the ground as guide lines.

6 To retain the subtlety of the marble, the effect produced in step 5 should not be overstated. So, immediately soften and blur it, and create further tonal variations, using the hog's hair softener.

7 To create the secondary veins, moisten a cotton bud with white spirit, and use it to wipe back the glaze to the white ground. These veins are tapered and angular, and cut across the panel without any particular reference to the features in the scumbled ground. Again, they should not be overstated.

8 The primary veins are sinewy, thread-like elements that follow convoluted paths over the ground, closely following the darker areas. Again, use a cotton bud moistened with white spirit to ciss the glaze. Then, prepare a rich yellow, transparent glaze by blending Indian red and yellow ochre with white spirit and scumble glaze. Using a fine artists' brush, introduce the glaze into the wiped-out primary veining channels. Roll the brush and splay the bristles to achieve the necessary tonal variations in colour along the length of the vein.

9 As a finishing touch, strengthen the primary veins by hardening-up their edges with copper powder mixed with a little white spirit. Apply this with a fine artists' brush. The effect should be subtle, and not overstated.

10 After the panel has thoroughly dried, apply one or two coats of mid-sheen or gloss polyurethane varnish.

Serpentine Marble

The Serpentine marbles are all characterised by the presence of the green mineral, serpentine. The tonal range of the hue is vast; from almost black, through the dark green and olives, and eventually to opaque white. Although each stone is identified by some specific characteristic, as a group they may be divided into three main visual categories.

The first type are the brecciated varieties. Stones such as 'vert antique', which have a familiar fractured appearance, are the darkest types. They have larger angular fragments, of black, green-grey and dark bottle-green, bedded in a light green to opaque-white matrix. The smaller white stones dotted around the ground tend to group in clusters.

The second main grouping are the swirling green and white types. Varieties such as 'verde issogne' exhibit swirling, white veining patterns, which flow over and totally dominate the mottled green ground beneath.

A third important type is vert de mer. This variety incorporates the best characteristics of both the other categories by balancing the strong presence of the veining system with the characteristic subtleties of the green hues. The satin-black ground is mottled with the dark tones of green and green-blue glazes, to produce the characteristic dense serpentine ground. Loosely constructed veining systems, superimposed in olive green, green-yellow and white, contrast with the ground and provide a feeling of depth and translucency

within the body of the stone.

While 'green marble' simulations must be used with restraint in the home in all but the largest rooms, they are successfully incorporated on wall surfaces as individually featured panels or contrasting border elements. The prominent white veining systems are particularly useful in directing the eye over or focusing the eye on featured surfaces, and in this respect 'book end' systems (see page 89) may be used to good effect in adjusting the visual proportions of a room. Horizontal surfaces such as tables and shelves are particularly suited to these effects.

MATERIALS
Artists' oils: white, veridian, oxide of chromium, raw umber
Black oil-based eggshell
Scumble glaze (flatting oil)
White (mineral) spirit
Polyurethane varnish (gloss)
4 cm (1½ in) standard flat brush
Hog's hair softening brush (medium)
Varnishing brush
A goose feather (or similar)
Stencil brush
Varnishing brush

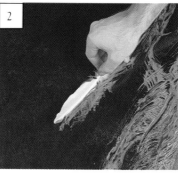

1 Apply a thin layer of scumble glaze to the entire surface of a black eggshell ground. Prepare a deep green glaze by blending veridian and raw umber with white spirit. Loosely stipple the colour over the surface, using a flat brush, and immediately soften it with a medium hog's hair softening brush. Allow this to dry for a few minutes.

2 Prepare a goose feather by splitting the fronds into variable sized sections, and moistening them with white spirit. Prepare a mid-green glaze by blending oxide of chromium with white spirit and a little scumble glaze. Using the feather, apply the glaze to the surface of the panel, with an imprecise, dithering motion. Try to strike a vague diagonal accent over the ground. It is a good idea when veining with a feather to first investigate its signature by practising on a trial board; when the feather is pulled in a straight line a strong, thin signature is displayed; where a sweeping motion is used, or the feather is driven at right

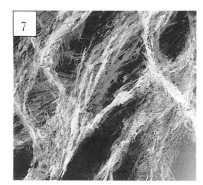

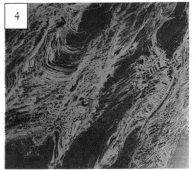

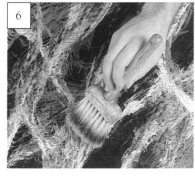

angles over the ground, the fronds separate into unpredictable sections and produce a variety of lines which vary both in thickness and intensity.

3 Before the green glaze dries, ciss it with white spirit: soak the stiff bristles of a stencil brush in the solvent, and pull your forefinger over the bristles to release fine droplets onto the surface of the panel. The glaze will disperse and open up to produce a varied and less regimented signature in the feathered veins.

4 The subtlety and depth of the superimposed green glazes becomes apparent as the surface dries out. Allow the panel to harden off for a few minutes, before the application of further glazes.

5 Prepare a transparent, white glaze by blending white artists' oil with white spirit and a little scumble glaze. Apply it to the surface using a feather, with an imprecise, dithering motion.

6 Lightly soften and blend the veins with the medium hog's hair softening brush. This will tone down some of the more strident markings.

7 It can be seen that some of the white veins roughly echo the directional flow in the underlying green ground; whilst others branch off at right angles, producing an element of tension in the composition.

Malachite

Malachite is a copper-bearing mineral that occurs naturally as a reniform or botryoidal mass; that is, either kidney shaped or similar in structure to a bunch of grapes. The latter form is most commonly used as a decorative stone.

When sectioned and polished, its emerald-green, banded parallels form complex, interconnected circular designs which are totally exclusive to this material. (In the past it was ground to form the inorganic pigment, 'mountain green'.) The silky lustre of the finish diffuses the semi-opaque bands of colour to produce an exquisite fantasy.

Although its rarity normally limits its use to small, polished slabs or delicate inlay work, in Russia the hall facings of the Winter Palace and the columns of St Isaac's Cathedral were made from malachite.

Where large masses of malachite occur, the closely related mineral azurite is often found at its core or centre. This equally decorative stone manifests itself in the form of brilliant blue, prismatic crystals.

Once again, it is most important, before commencing a simulation, to have a rough sketched design to work from. Whilst the flowing patterns may appear simple to reproduce, it can be difficult to organise the effect into a satisfactory composition.

However, the bold patterning of malachite provides endless inspirational possibilities for the creation of fantasy finishes. The patterns are easily reproduced using all manner of homemade combs. The skill lies in selecting the most effective colour contrast between the ground coat and banding.

Subtle patterning can be produced by featuring pale, translucent pastels against a white ground. For more stunning effects, use opaque colours and sharp contrasts – fluorescent paints featured against a matt-black ground can be visually compelling.

Although as a fantasy simulation malachite may be applied to almost any surface, as an authentic reproduction it is best displayed as a semi-precious material on table tops, panel surrounds or tiled mosaics.

MATERIALS
Artists' oils: veridian, raw umber
Turquoise oil-based eggshell
Scumble glaze
(flatting oil)
White (mineral) spirit
Polyurethane varnish (mid-sheen)
2.5 cm (1 in) standard flat brush
Hog's hair softening brush
Varnishing brush
Semi-rigid card
Scissors
Cotton buds (Q-tips)
Pencil eraser
Clean, lint-free cloth

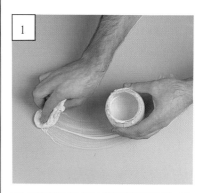

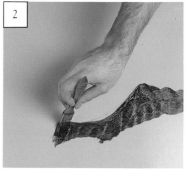

1 *Paint the panel with an opaque ground of turquoise oil-based eggshell. When dry, apply a thin layer of scumble glaze, using a clean cloth.*

2 *Prepare a dark green glaze by blending veridian and raw umber with white spirit and a little scumble glaze. Using a small flat brush, roughly apply the glaze to the area that will represent the major spine of the marble – work with a sketch or photo for reference.*

Now with a dabbing action, use a hog's hair softener to gently soften the green glaze, and disguise the brushmarks.

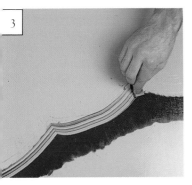

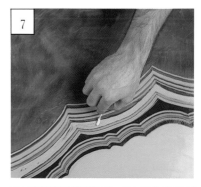

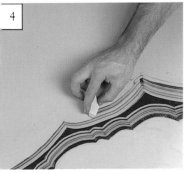

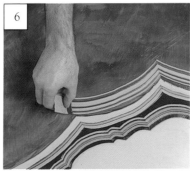

3 Prepare a piece of semi-rigid card as a comb, by roughly tearing it over a straight edge and cutting it to a width of 2.5 cm (1 in) to 5 cm (2 in). After testing its signature on a spare piece of paper, pull the comb through the glaze in a continuous sweep, to produce the parallel curved sections.

4 Tidy up the edges of the curved sections, or bays, by wiping back the glaze to a clean, hard edge, using a pencil eraser.

5 Prepare a deep green glaze by blending veridian with white spirit. Apply it to the panel, making sure its edge roughly follows the shape of the curved sections in the central spine. Lightly soften the glaze with a medium hog's hair softening brush.

6 Prepare another comb from the semi-rigid card; this time cutting out more defined sections in the rough edge, so that wider areas will remain undisturbed when the comb is dragged through the glaze. After testing its signature, roughly follow the contours of the bays, distressing the glaze in a series of continuous, steady, arcing movements.

7 Where the lines overlap, or become messy and confused, tidy them by mopping up stray glaze with a cotton bud.

8 The major arcing parallels are now created using a larger comb prepared from the semi-rigid card (as described in step 4). Remember to test its signature. This time, create more pronounced and dramatic features by accentuating the vertical travel of the card through the glaze. Move systematically across the panel in a clockwise, continuous and flowing motion.

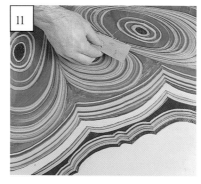

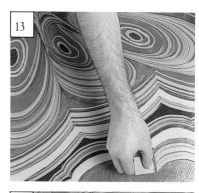

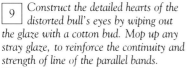

9 Construct the detailed hearts of the distorted bull's eyes by wiping out the glaze with a cotton bud. Mop up any stray glaze, to reinforce the continuity and strength of line of the parallel bands.

10 Strengthen the centres of the distorted bull's eyes by painting in a deep green glaze; created by blending veridian and raw umber with white spirit.

11 To complete the outer areas of the bull's eyes, use the comb employed in step 9 to make a series of arcing, anti-clockwise sweeps.

12 The upper part of the panel is now painted in with the dark green glaze prepared in step 2. Once again, use the brush strokes to emphasise the rough, curving sweeps of the bays.

13 Prepare a small comb, and after testing its signature pull it through the wet glaze, to produce sympathetic parallels that echo the curves of the central spine.

14 Finally, when the panel has dried protect the finish, and simulate the lustrous, waxy appearance of Malachite, by applying one or two coats of mid-sheen polyurethane varnish.

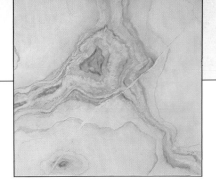

Yellow Onyx

The most attractive varieties of onyx feature a series of exquisitely toned parallels and banded strata, whose appearance closely resembles the patterns found in wood grain.

To continue the analogy: in a tree the parallels are the sectioned annual growth rings of the trunk and branching structures; in sectioned onyx the bands are produced by the progressive dehydration of hot solutions, and the subsequent deposition and crystalisation of coloured solids. Features evident in timber – distended heartwood, darkly stated knots and fine-banded growth rings – are also clearly visible in the surface of the polished stone.

The background bruising effect commonly found in onyx produces the characteristic translucency. The banded parallels congregate and flow in lighter channels, towards and around islands of darkly stated opaque colour, which form the dominant features of the overall marble pattern.

Onyx marbles generally exhibit one colour, which tends to be understated, and the visual strength of the stone relies on the subtle tonal gradations that are produced within the patterning.

The stones tend to be fragile, and the darker coloured islands are often crossed by dramatic stress fractures, which travel over the ground dis- locating the surrounding banded parallels.

Onyx is one of the most decorative and highly prized stones. It is often used in the preparation of ornaments, ornament bases and table tops. Although it shows excellent translucent qualities, the strength and complexity of the pattern is usually so compelling that its use as a wall-cladding material is restricted to all but the largest of rooms.

MATERIALS
White oil-based eggshell
Artists' oils: burnt Sienna, yellow ochre, ultramarine, white
Scumble glaze (flatting oil)
White (mineral) spirit
Polyurethane varnish (mid-sheen)
2.5 cm (1 in) standard flat brush
Hog's hair softening brush (small)
Artists' brushes (medium and fine)
Pencil eraser
Clean, lint-free cloth

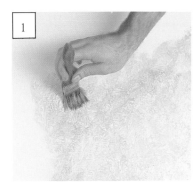

1 Wipe a thin layer of neat scumble glaze over the entire surface of the white eggshell ground, using a clean cloth. Prepare some glazes by blending burnt Sienna, ultramarine and white with white spirit. Produce a variety of tones, varying from deep orange-brown to pale, violet-grey brown, by slightly altering the proportions of the ingredients.
Stipple the glazes onto the panel, with a flat brush, and roughly merge the colours where they meet.

2 Immediately soften the glazes by striking the panel in all directions with a hog's hair softening brush. The panel will now exhibit the characteristic mottled and tonally gradated appearance of the marble.

Note that the success of the finished simulation heavily depends on the soft, tonal gradations of colour produced in Steps 1 and 2; and that the prominent yellow/brown area is the basis for the focal point of the composition – so its position must be accurately determined with reference to a sketch or photo.

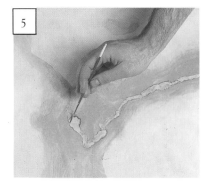

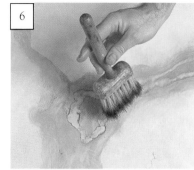

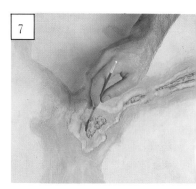

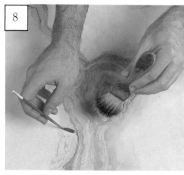

3 │ *After the panel has dried overnight, wipe a thin layer of scumble glaze over the ground, using a cloth. Prepare a deep, orange-brown glaze by blending burnt Sienna and ultramarine with white spirit and a little scumble glaze. Apply the glaze to the area of yellow background, using a small, flat brush. The rough, spine-like shape will later generate the concentric, blurred parallels that are characteristic of the onyx marbles.*

4 │ *Soften the glaze with a hog's hair softening brush.*

5 │ *Blend some transparent and tonally varied glazes, by tinting yellow ochre with the colour produced in step 1. Apply them with an artists' brush, in concentric bands that reinforce the shape of the central spine.*

6 │ *Soften the bands with a hog's hair softener, but only lightly, as the crude drag marks created by the flat brush will help establish the flowing qualities of the pattern.*

7 │ *While the glazes remain workable, pull a fine artists' brush, loaded with white spirit and a little scumble glaze, through the colour in a direction that roughly compliments the parallel banding. It is advisable to ciss the channels from the centre, working outwards.*

8 │ *Immediately soften the cissed channels by striking across them with a hog's hair softener.*

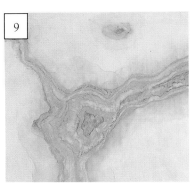

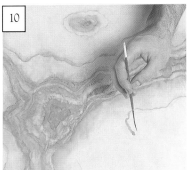

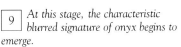

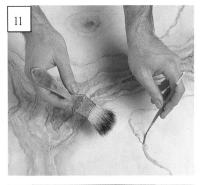

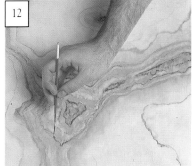

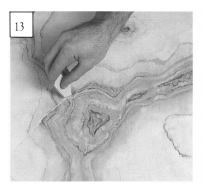

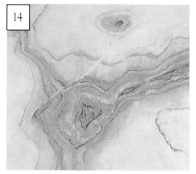

9   At this stage, the characteristic blurred signature of onyx begins to emerge.

10   Produce a deep brown glaze by blending yellow ochre, burnt Sienna and ultramarine with a little white spirit and scumble glaze. Apply it sparingly, using a fine artists' brush, to create and reinforce the parallel bands.
Alternate between lighter and darker, and more and less opaque versions of the glaze, and continually soften the effect. Continue the process until all the parallels are completed around the central feature. Note, that at the edge of the spine the coloured bands should become so transparent they begin to merge into the mottled ground.

11   Employ the darker glaze used in stage 10 to identify thin bands of colour on the extremities of the spine, which do not conform to the strict parallel patterning; and also use it to strengthen isolated elements in the mottled ground, such as the bull's eye. Immediately soften them with the hog's hair softener.

12   Use this dark glaze, on a fine artists' brush, to harden-up and emphasise detail within the central spine.

13   Whilst onyx is extremely beautiful, it is essentially a soft material prone to structural faults. These appear as traumatic gashes that cut across and disjoint the banded strata.
Simulate them by wiping back the glaze to the scumbled ground, using the clean, hard edge of a pencil eraser; but do not overstate them.

14   When the panel is dry, apply one or two coats of mid-sheen polyurethane varnish for a lustrous and protected finish.

Rhodocrosite

A highly prized, manganese-bearing mineral, rhodocrosite occurs in the form of large, beautiful, pink to blood-red crystals. Some of these can be up to 5 cm (2 in) in length. The crystals are organised into fine parallel bands, which may vary in width from 6 cm (2¼ in) to a fine pinstripe, and are featured against a pale yellow to white ground. The overall pattern may be gently undulating, convoluted or roughly circular in form.

The stone is translucent, and the polished surface can vary from highly reflective to a dull, pearly lustre. Because of its rarity value, the polished stone is used sparingly – usually on table tops, or featured as inlay material on walls, set against less expensive stones. As small panels or tiles the banded strata can be used decoratively to produce intricate mosaics, or the more formal 'book-end' type patterning.

As with all stones that exhibit a strident pattern, care must be taken to see that it does not dominate those areas where it is applied.

MATERIALS

White oil-based eggshell
Artists' oils: Alizarin crimson, chrome yellow, yellow ochre, white
Scumble glaze (flatting oil)
White (mineral) spirit
Polyurethane varnish (mid-sheen)
Rubbing compound
4 cm (1½ in) flat brush
Hog's hair softening brush
Artists' pencil (fine)
Hexagonal-sectioned pencil
Semi-rigid card
Clean, lint-free cloth
Medium angled fitch
Varnishing brush
Muslin cloth

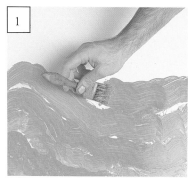

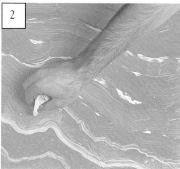

1 *Prepare a deep pink glaze by blending Alizarin crimson, chrome yellow and white with white spirit and scumble glaze. Apply it to the white eggshell ground in rough parallel bands, using a flat brush in broad, undulating sweeps. Vary the width of the bands, and slightly alter their tone by varying the mix of the glaze. Cover the entire panel, leaving just the odd slash of background white showing through.*

2 *Using a clean cloth, wipe out banded sections of the glaze. Vary their width, and follow the directional flow of the strata – until the entire ground is covered with alternating bands of pink and white parallels.*

3 *Prepare a transparent yellow glaze by blending yellow ochre with white spirit and scumble glaze. Apply this to the white parallels, using a medium, angled fitch. Vary the transparency of the glaze, by altering the ratio of scumble to colour. You will find that the yellow glaze will merge with remnants of pink remaining in the wiped-out white channels to produce pleasing variations in colour.*

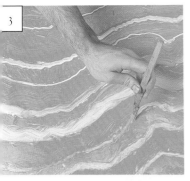

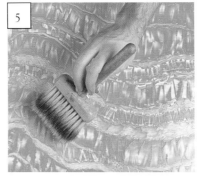

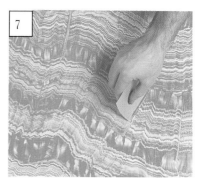

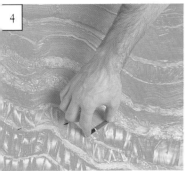

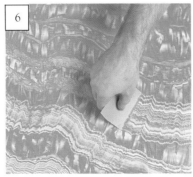

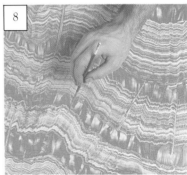

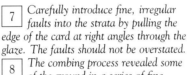

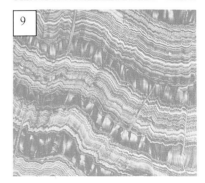

4 To simulate the rhodochrosite crystals, dab and smear the red-bands with a short length of pencil. Vary the print, but keep the directional accent of the crystals more or less at right angles to the flow of the strata.

5 Lightly soften and blend the crystal formations by striking the panel in all directions with a hog's hair softener. The numerous tonal variations produced by this technique will contribute substantially to the subtlety of the finish.

6 Pieces of semi-rigid card are used to create the beautiful, dithering parallels that are a particular feature of the stone. Prepare several samples, varying in length between 2.5 cm (1 in) and 10 cm (4 in), by tearing them along a straight edge. Test the signature of their fine, irregular teeth on a spare piece of paper.

Now, pull a comb through the wet glaze in a continuous, dithering motion – closely following the parallel direction of the strata. Pull combs of varying lengths through the glaze, but leave some sections of the crystalised strata undisturbed.

7 Carefully introduce fine, irregular faults into the strata by pulling the edge of the card at right angles through the glaze. The faults should not be overstated.

8 The combing process revealed some of the ground in a series of fine, white parallel channels. Using a fine artists' brush, introduce a transparent yellow glaze of yellow ochre, white spirit and scumble into some of the more prominent channels, and strengthen existing yellow bands.

9 When the panel has dried, apply one or two coats of mid-sheen polyurethane varnish. Finally, when the varnish has dried, polish the surface with a medium grade rubbing compound and muslin cloth. This will simulate the waxy, lustrous finish of the polished stone.

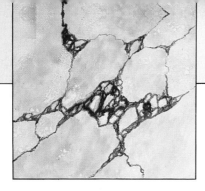

Fantasy White Vein Marble

The classic white vein marble (see pages 100-1) lends itself to fantasy effects. Provided the ground colours remain translucent (pale pastels, for example), any number of fantasies can be created by scumbling and veining over them in two or three different shades of the same colour. The finish is suitable for most surfaces, provided that the pattern isn't over-stated. Prominent, exaggerated patterns are best used on features such as fire surrounds or table tops.

Since fantasy finishes are impressionistic in nature, they are particularly suited to the water-based marbling system (see page 56), where speed is of the essence.

MATERIALS

**White oil-based eggshell
Artists' oils: black, raw umber, burnt umber, yellow ochre
White (mineral) spirit
Scumble glaze (flatting oil)
Oil-based crayons: black and dark grey
Polyurethane varnish (gloss or mid-sheen)
2.5 cm (1 in) standard flat brush
Hog's hair softening brush (small)
Varnishing brush
Clean, lint-free cloth
Natural marine sponge**

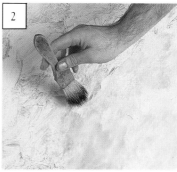

1 *Apply a thin layer of neat scumble glaze to the white eggshell ground, using a clean cloth. Prepare a number of dirty yellow-grey glazes by blending varying proportions of raw umber, yellow ochre, burnt umber and black with white spirit. Take the glazes up on a standard flat brush, and roughly stipple them onto the panel with an imprecise dabbing action.*

2 *Immediately soften and blend the glazes with a small hog's hair softener – encouraging any interesting formations in the scumbled ground. Note that the disposition of the darker grey glazes on the panel will establish the position of the prominent elements in the design, such as the major veining channels.*

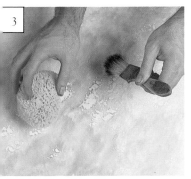

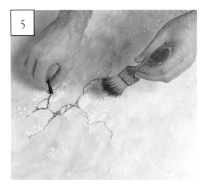

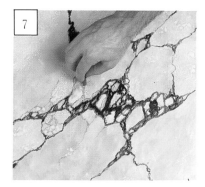

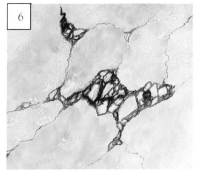

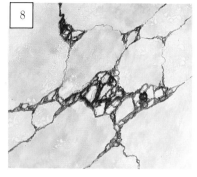

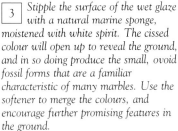

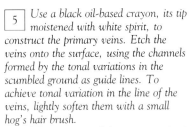

3 Stipple the surface of the wet glaze with a natural marine sponge, moistened with white spirit. The cissed colour will open up to reveal the ground, and in so doing produce the small, ovoid fossil forms that are a familiar characteristic of many marbles. Use the softener to merge the colours, and encourage further promising features in the ground.

Be careful with the cissing technique, as once more the resulting features will determine the location and course of the primary and secondary veins.

4 When the panel is dry, apply a thin layer of scumble glaze to the scumbled ground.

5 Use a black oil-based crayon, its tip moistened with white spirit, to construct the primary veins. Etch the veins onto the surface, using the channels formed by the tonal variations in the scumbled ground as guide lines. To achieve tonal variation in the line of the veins, lightly soften them with a small hog's hair brush.

6 The signature of the primary veins is enhanced by strengthening selected portions with the crayon. Detailed, angular sections enclose defined fragments of colour in the ground, and less powerfully stated lines link these areas.

7 Now introduce the secondary veins onto the panel, using a dark grey crayon. These veins are understated, and move out from the regions of the primary veins to occupy the more remote and paler areas of the panel.

8 When the surface has dried out, apply one or two coats of mid-sheen or gloss polyurethane varnish for protection.

Figures in italics refer to illustrations

acrylic matt medium 71
acrylic paints 57, 58
additive method 64
alabasters 16
alcoves *24*, 92
antiquing 28
artefacts 28, 34, 50-2, 82, 93
artists' oils 57, 59
azurite 116

bathrooms 42-6
bedrooms 40-1
belgian red *20*
black and gold marble 102-3
bois jourdan 112-13
book-end patterning *44*, 88, 89,
    89
borders 92
breccias 16, 106
breche pernise *32*
breche rose *44*
breche violet 110-11
broken colour techniques 9,
    64-75
brushes 56
    and veining 73-4

Carrara marbles 16
ceilings *26*, 30, *44*
cissing 68-70, *68*, *69*
classical themes 28, 53
cloudiness of marble 99
colour
    characteristics 60-1, *60*, *61*
    qualities 96-8
colour washing 67-8, *68*
combing 66, *66*

demountable system 86
density of pattern 24
depth of marble 99
detergent, liquid 58
dippers 59
direct system 86
discordant colours 61
distressing 64
domestic uses 24-53
doors 26, 33, 40, 47
dragging 10, *24*, *47*, 66, *66*

failures 21
fantasy, abstract 29
fantasy white vein marble 124-5
feathers 74
fibreglass, preparation 82-3
fidgeting 74
filler *79*
fireplaces 38-9, 91
flatting oil 58
floor panels 91-3
floorboards 81-2
floors *24*, 32, 37, 41, 49, *90*,
    91, 91-3
    preparation 80-2, *81*
formation of marble 15-18
fringing 68
furniture 34, 41, 50-2, 93
    preparation 82

gardens 53
geology of marble 15-18
gilp 59
glass, preparation 82
glazes 57-60
glycerine 56
gouache 56, 58
granites 15, 65, *67*

greenhouses 53
grounds 58, 59
    eggshell 99
    preparation 78-83
    scumbled 70
gypsums 16

halls 30-3
historical aspects 8-9, 19-20, 28

illusions 21, 24, 96
inlay work 93
intensity 60
isolating 71-2

Kershaw, Thomas *18-21*, *20*
kitchens 47-9

limestones 16
lineoleum paint 80, *81*
linseed oil 57, 59
living areas 34-7

malachite 66, 116-8
melamine surfaces 47
metal, preparation 83
mistakes 88
motion of marble 99

Acknowledgements

Picture credits

Arcaid/Richard Bryant: 24, 46t.
Brigitte Baert/Alain Dovifat: 42, 44, 45t.
B. C. Sanitan/Sheila Fitzjones P. R.: 47, 49t.
By kind permission of Bolton Corporation, Bolton Museum: 18, 19, 20, 21.
Michael Boys: 23, 33, 37b, 39t.
Paul Brierly: 14, 116l.
Courtauld Institute: 7.
Courtesy of Davies Keeling and Trowbridge: 53.
Michael Holford: 10.
Angelo Hornak: 32t (marbler Mark Hornak).
Courtesy of House and Garden/Duncan McNeil: 51 (marbler Michael Daly).
Macdonald Orbis: 15, 16, 25, 31, 41, 45b, 46b, 48, 49c, 52, 62, 63, 66-75,
96, 97, 98, 100-1, 102-3, 104r, 106r, 107, 108r, 109, 110r, 111, 112r, 113,
114r, 115, 116r, 117, 118, 119r, 120, 121, 122r, 123, 124, 125.
Macdonald Orbis/Courtesy of Whitehead & Sons Ltd: 100t, 102l, 104l,
106l, 108l, 110l, 114l, 122l.
Maison de Marie-Claire/Serge Korniloff: 37t.
Ronald Sheridan: 8, 9.
Smallbone/Sheila Fitzjones P. R.: 47, 49t.
Trio Design Ltd: 55 (painter Michael Snyder)
Fritz von der Schulenburg: 26, 27 © Interiors, 34, 35, 36.
Elizabeth Whiting & Associates: 30, 40, 49b.
P. Woloszynski: 32b, 38, 50.
World of Interiors/James Mortimer: 39b.

Stuart Spencer would like to thank: all the staff at Macdonald for their hard work
on this book, and Henryk Terpilowski for his help and advice on the art of marbling.